Boomer Shock

Preparing Communities
for the Retirement Generation

By Ellen Hirsch de Haan, ESQ.

With a Case Study by Arthur W. Brown

Community Associations Press
Alexandria, VA

ISBN 0-944715-78-8
Boomer Shock: Preparing Communities for the Retirement Generation
© 2004 Community Associations Press, a division of Community Associations Institute.

Community Associations Press
A Division of Community Associations Institute
225 Reinekers Lane, Ste. 300
Alexandria, VA 22314

To order additional copies of this book, please write to the publisher at the address above or call (703) 548-8600. You can also order online at *www.caionline.org/bookstore.cfm*.

This publication is designed to provide accurate and authoritative information in regard to the subject matter covered. It is sold with the understanding that the publisher is not engaged in rendering legal, accounting, or other professional services. If legal advice or other expert assistance is required, the services of a competent professional should be sought.
> —From a Declaration of Principles, jointly adopted by a Committee of the American Bar Association and a Committee of Publishers

Printed in the United States of America

Library of Congress Cataloging-in-Publication Data

Haan, Ellen de.
    Boomer shock : preparing communities for the retirement generation /by Ellen Hirsch de Haan, Esq. with a case study by Arthur W. Brown.–
        1st ed.
        p. cm.
    ISBN 0-944715-78-8
1. Aged–United States. 2. Baby boom generation–Retirement–United States. 3. Aged–Services for–United States. I. Brown, Arthur W. II. Title.
    HQ1064.U5H14 20047
    305.26'0973–dc22

                                2003025776

Contents

Acknowledgments

AUTHOR
Ellen Hirsch de Haan, ESQ.

CASE STUDY AUTHOR
Arthur W. Brown

EDITOR
Debra H. Lewin, Director
Community Associations Press

CONTRIBUTOR
Paul D. Grucza, CMCA, AMS, PCAM
Consolidated Community
Management, AAMC
Tamarac, FL

REVIEWERS
Samuel L. Dolnick
Lake Park Condominium
LaMesa, CA

Robert A. Felix, CMCA, LSM, PCAM
Consolidated Community
Services, LLC
Denver, CO

Paul D. Grucza, CMCA, AMS, PCAM
Consolidated Community
Management, AAMC
Tamarac, FL

Beverly Scenna
Highlands Lake HOA
Palm Harbor, FL

CAI gratefully acknowledges the members and leaders of Del Mesa Carmel, especially General Manager Joseph Begbie, for sharing their experiences and allowing us to publish their story.

Preface

Bulletin: A tidal wave is approaching America, and it will break over the country in about 2011. That's the year Baby Boomers will begin retiring, and the demographic face of America will change inexorably. When that happens, the nature of our communities will change as well. Associations can react when they're swamped by that wave, or they can begin their preparations now. Consider the latest projections from the U.S. Bureau of the Census, the Social Security Administration, and the Department of Health and Human Services.

Greater Numbers

The proportion of seniors in America is already higher than it's ever been—13 percent. But, within a few short years—around 2011—that number will increase dramatically to 20 percent as the Baby Boomers—people born between 1946–1964—reach age 65. The U.S. Department of Health and Human Services projects that by 2030, one of every five Americans will be over the age of 65. Eleven percent of the U.S. population will be between ages 65 and 75, and nine percent will be over 75.

Longer Lives

Baby Boomers will swell the ranks of the population over age 65, and they will be with us longer than any other demographic group in the nation's history thanks to improved nutrition, advanced health care, and eradication and control of disease that have come about during their lifetimes. Consequently, between 2011 and 2030, the number of seniors over 85 will increase faster than those who are 65–84. According to the Administration on Aging, "The cumulative growth in the 85-and-over population from 1995 to 2050 is anticipated to be more than 400 percent."

Increased Ethnic Diversity

Not only will the number of people over 65 increase, but the racial composition of this group will also change dramatically. Between 1995 and 2030, Blacks over the age of 65 will increase by 155 percent; Hispanics over 65 will increase by 417 percent; and "other races"—to use the Census Bureau's term—over 65 will increase by 380 percent. The number of Whites over 65, on the other hand, will trail with an increase of 95 percent.

Decreased Support

By 2011, one American in five will have special needs, and the number of Americans available to provide for them—directly or indirectly—will be smaller than ever before. In 2000, for every 10 people between the ages of 18 and 64 (presumably wage earning, productive adults), there were approximately six "dependents" (people under 18 or over 65). By 2020, that number increases to approximately seven dependents, and by 2030, to almost eight dependents for every ten wage earners.

Increased Needs

On top of all this, a report titled "Aging into the 21st Century," prepared by the Department of Health and Human Services, predicts that "There will be large increases by 2030 in the numbers [of elderly] requiring special services in housing, transportation, recreation, and education, as well as health and nutrition." Note that the first item on this list is housing. The need for special services in housing will have significant meaning for community associations during the next three decades.

Meeting Needs

"Aging into the 21st Century" goes on to say that "The need and cost of support of dependent elderly can be mitigated by substituting . . . family, friends, and *neighbors* as caregivers for private caregivers. . . . Some groups in our society have gone further than others in the use of family members, friends, and *neighbors* as caregivers." [Emphasis added.] If community associations are not among those impacted by this trend now, they soon will be. The report concludes: "These prospective demographic changes have given rise to a general concern about the social, economic, and physical 'health' of our nation's population." Community associations should be equally concerned about how these changes will affect the social and economic health of their associations.

This book is intended to get community association boards, managers, and professionals to think about—perhaps even worry about—the inevitable, and then to actively prepare for it.

CHAPTER 1

Today's Realities

Baby Boomers will never concede they're old. And why should they, when life expectancies are increasing steadily and experts are predicting further advances? For example, Ken Dychtwald, a psychologist and author, believes that new developments in organ cloning, availability of cyborg body parts, and biotechnological manipulations of biological clocks may allow Baby Boomers to live well past 100—looking and feeling like 50- and 60-year-olds.

At a meeting of researchers at the University of California School of Medicine in 1999, Steve Austad, a University of Idaho biologist, said he believed there's a 75 percent chance that someone born in the late 1990's will live to be 150. Cynthia Kenyon, a professor of biochemistry and biophysics at the University of California-San Francisco, predicts that we can look ahead to 90-year-olds who are as functional as 50-year-olds. Clearly, the definition of "old" will change dramatically in the coming years.

These predictions aren't as far-fetched as they might seem. In the 15 years between 1980 and 1995, the number of Americans living longer than 100 years tripled. And, according to the US Census Bureau, by the year 2020, there will be a 14 percent increase in the number of people over the age of 80. According to Census 2000, men are living longer than ever before. And, men's survival past age 65 is increasing faster than women's, which may be a function of the full participation of women in what was once a man's world of business and bread-winning.

Retirement, and retirement communities, as we think of them today, very likely will no longer exist in 50 years. Instead, there will simply be communities with diverse age groups, income levels, races, cultures, and family status. And they will likely be covenant-controlled communities—yours. (For a more detailed examination of the association of the future, see Appendix 1.)

But that's the future. Today's reality is that there are four generations who are trying to live together.

Diversity
Matures

The Matures were born between 1920 and 1945. They're the last of the veterans of the World and Korean Wars, and are also called the "Silent Generation." This generation is all about sacrifice. They survived the Great Depression, and now they still reuse aluminum foil and paper bags. Their heroes were military figures. They believe that a rule is a rule. They feel that change is good, as long as it's the type of change they've envisioned. The Matures defined the world in which we live for many years, but they now have to give way to the Baby Boomers.

Baby Boomers

Baby Boomers were born between 1946 and 1964. Approximately 77 million in number, this group is made up of workaholics who believe in teamwork and democracy. They don't take sick days, and they value loyalty. They don't necessarily see the need to follow rules. Their heroes tend to be national figures, like John F. Kennedy and Martin Luther King. Until approximately 2030, we will continue to have Baby Boomer Presidents in the White House.

Baby Boomers share with the Matures a sense of history and the value of craftsmanship, the concept of "built to last." They invented the idea of "meaningful work," and the workplace continues to be a part of their self-identity.

Generation X

Generation X'ers were born between 1965 and 1977. Numbering about 44 million, this group was raised in an environment in which both parents worked. They question their parents' values, and they believe that jobs and housing are disposable. This generation places greater value on family and personal life than the Baby Boomers do, and they feel that a balanced life is more important than professional accomplishments.

Generation Y

Generation Y's, also called the Echo Boomers, were born between 1977 and 2000. They number about 80 million and comprise approximately 33 percent of the U.S. population. For the first time in nearly half a century, the Baby Boomers are no longer the largest population segment. And Generation Y is only going to get larger. Projections suggest that by the year 2010, those age 33 and younger will number 137 million, or 46 percent of the U.S. population.

People in this group have been protected and provided for. Many of them have always known the Internet, laptops, and cell phones. It would never occur to them to physically touch a television to change the channel.

People born in the U.S. after 1983 have always had a President from the Southern states in office. South Africa's official policy of apartheid has not existed in their lifetime. For them, cars have always had CD players and air bags, and weather reports have always been available 24 hours a day on television. To Generation Y, the United States and Russia have always been partners in space, a hotline is a consumer service, rather than a red phone used to avoid an accidental nuclear war, and genetic testing and DNA screening have always been available.

This generation focuses on its individual choices, goals, and future. Savvy marketers appeal to this generation as individuals—such as the military recruitment ad that touts the "Army of One." For them, the work ethic is equivalent to the worth ethic.

What does this generational diversity mean for community associations?

Where these generations mix in a community association, there is a potential for tension arising from differing approaches to life, work, and values—but only if association leaders and managers ignore the differences between the demographics.

Recognizing and accommodating these differences and being sensitive to the flash points will enable associations to take advantages of the strengths of each of these groups. For example, Matures would be better suited for organizing a community rummage sale rather than Gen X, and Gen Y would be more likely to successfully develop a community website than a Baby Boomer. Admittedly, these are broad generalizations, but keeping these generational profiles in mind will aid associations in planning, decision making, and problem solving.

Age is only one aspect of diversity within community associations today. Part of the strength of this country is that it was built on racial and ethnic diversity right from inception. The future will bring a larger diversity of population within community associations, and a variety of cultural and ethnic backgrounds.

Consider, for example, that in 2000, 5.4 percent of the elderly population was Hispanic; and the Administration on Aging projects a percentage increase to 17.5 by 2050. Similar rates of increase are expected for Blacks, Asians, and other non-White races. On the other hand, the percent of elderly who are White will decrease from 90 to 82 percent. In short, over the next 50 years, the number of elderly non-Whites will steadily increase to about 33 percent. Clearly, the racial and ethnic composition of the elderly population in the U.S. will change profoundly in the next few decades; and the nature of the community associations in which they live will need to change in order to remain a viable housing arrangement. What kind of changes might associations begin thinking about?

- The new diversity of our communities will bring new challenges in creating a sense of community in which all residents understand the requirements that must be met to allow everyone to share living spaces.

- We will have a diversity of use, activities, and design in our communities, arising from and in response to our diverse populations.

- We will recognize the inherent social tensions of trying to balance people and property, and the social tensions which are created by diversity, and we will use them to create a balance and to focus on relationships, rather than on compliance.

- We will look for the shared common traits and goals, not for the differences.

- We will strive for flexible design to provide packages of amenities and incorporate an inclusive lifestyle, not an exclusionary community.

Until these outcomes are realized, there will be more immediate practical considerations for community associations. The unfortunate reality for minorities in the U.S. is that they tend to exist at a lower economic level than Whites. Presumably, that will improve as we move further into the 21st century. However, in the short term, community associations can expect—not only a growing elderly population—but a greater number of non-White elderly. These residents will have fewer economic resources. That cloud's silver lining is that non-Whites tend to have larger extended families and stronger social connections, a fact that associations should make the most of when meeting the needs their ethnic residents.

Decline and Disability

Over the next few decades, community associations will need to prepare and make accommodations for a rapidly increasing number of residents in poor health and residents who are disabled.

Both the Census Bureau and the Office of the Actuary of the Social Security Administration project that a larger proportion of the population is likely to survive to very advanced age in the first half of the 21st century. Furthermore, studies conducted by the University of Illinois at Chicago and the University of Chicago project the number of elderly with poor health will increase sharply from 1990 to 2030. Black elderly in poor health by 2030 would be triple the number in 1990.

Emergency Procedures

Community volunteers and professional managers should develop programs and create specific procedures for handling age-related emergencies. This should be published and made available to all volunteer leaders and staff, as well as any residents who would like a copy.

Emergency procedure manuals are not uncommon in community associations. But are the special needs of the over-65 population included? Associations should review or implement emergency procedures with these special considerations in mind. For example, are procedures in place for providing information on medication to a paramedic?

Having such procedures in place before they are actually needed enables the association to respond quickly and efficiently with action appropriate to the emergency.

Decline

Deterioration in residents' abilities is inevitable with age. For those living alone, this simple reality can be a big problem. According to the U.S. Census Bureau, in 2000, nearly 31 percent of women between ages 65 and 74 lived alone. For those over 75, 49 percent lived alone. Among men between the ages of 65 and 74, nearly 14 percent lived alone, and of those over 75, 21 percent lived alone.

Therefore, while decline isn't an "emergency," procedures for dealing with declining health and ability should be included in an association's procedures manual. For example, a system of monitoring residents' well being—especially residents who live alone—on a frequent and regular basis would be an appropriate procedure. Similarly, systems that offer support in the aftermath of catastrophic illness would be beneficial. For example:

- Organize a community buddy system in which residents check on homebound residents or those living alone. This type of monitoring can prevent difficult situations from escalating into real emergencies, and can actually save a life. It will add immeasurably to the quality of life of both the senior resident and the person providing the service, who has the opportunity to make a difference in someone's life.

- Appoint a committee to make periodic and regular calls to family members of seniors. Staying in touch keeps the family involved, lets them know the association cares about mom's or dad's well being, and makes it harder for family members to "warehouse" a senior with the association. In addition, this type of relationship building makes it easier for the association to turn to the family when emergencies arise.

- Appoint a committee to provide companion services—similar to babysitting—to spouses or children of incapacitated residents. This provides relief from their caretaker role so they can shop, run errands, or just have some personal time.

Disabilities

An article in the *Journal of Gerontology: Social Sciences* projects that the number of elderly people with disabilities will increase dramatically by 2040.

- In 2020, the number of Americans age 65 and older with *moderate* disabilities (defined as impaired ability to carry on the activities of daily living, such as eating, dressing, bathing, and cleaning) will approach 10 million—that's a 68 percent increase from 1990 to 2020.

- In 1990, 3.8 million people age 65 and above had *severe* disabilities, including those with Alzheimer's. By 2040 the number is projected to jump to 14.3 million people, and of these 70 percent will be 85 or older.

Although modern science has limited the nature and severity of disabilities, the sheer number of people approaching and exceeding age 65 in the next few years will outstrip any advances. The result will be that the number of elderly residents with moderate or sever disabilities will nearly triple by 2040.

Furthermore, the risk of becoming disabled is greater among lower income populations. Nearly three-quarters of elderly who are disabled have incomes near the poverty level.

For community associations, an awareness of the protections offered by federal regulations to disabled residents—particularly Fair Housing regulations—will be crucial.

Fair Housing

Even in the face of recently published data, there are still very few laws that directly address the issues of aging at the federal, state, or local levels in the U.S. However, the federal Fair Housing Amendments Act of 1988, which prohibits discrimination against persons who are mentally or physically handicapped—conditions frequently experienced by older people—should not be ignored by associations.

In many cases, the natural effects of aging render older residents mentally or physically handicapped. These individuals may need to modify their homes or be exempted from certain rules in order to access or enjoy their homes—including the common areas. Therefore, Fair Housing regulations require community associations to allow reasonable modifications to common areas and common elements, at the expense of the handicapped individual, to allow them to access and enjoy the amenities.

Parking and Fair Housing

Parking is an issue commonly affected by Fair Housing requirements, and it brings a number of practical problems for associations when individuals request a permanent handicapped parking space. Reserving a handicapped parking space is required under the reasonable accommodation requirements of the Act.

However, if an association has assigned parking spaces, then the right to use the space belongs to the unit, and it cannot be taken away from an owner without his or her agreement. If the spaces earmarked for assignment as handicapped spaces—perhaps because they are closest to the door of the handicapped resident—are already assigned, the association cannot reassign them, under most documents.

At some point, as more and more residents grow older and qualify for these spaces, there may be more requests than available spaces. The Fair Housing Amendments Act is strictly applied; and, whenever possible, association leaders and managers should make every effort to accommodate requests for reserved handicapped parking from residents who qualify. For example:

- Make arrangements with neighbors for voluntary exchanges of spaces.

- Swap guest, unassigned, or employee parking spaces, if possible.

- Free up spaces by instructing employees to park in commercial lots where possible, and let the association absorb the expense as a normal cost of doing business.

Mixed Age Communities

When communities are made up of a mixed age population, tension can arise between the needs and interests of young families with children and retired individuals. For example, if the association provides facilities for children, then these facilities must be fully and regularly maintained.

Likewise, any rules and regulations governing use of the facilities and the dwellings must be reasonable, and uniformly applied to all residents, regardless of their age, in order to be enforceable under federal fair housing laws. This would include regulations regarding playing music and electronic equipment; noise; and use of recreational amenities, such as the swimming pool, ping-pong tables, and so on.

Rules and regulations and members' fiduciary responsibilities on behalf of the *whole* community are of particular concern in a mixed age community because of possible claims of discrimination based on familial status (families with children), under the federal laws. Check with the association's attorney if any aspects of these regulations are unclear.

Difficult Behavior

Gradual loss of mental acuity is a natural concomitant of the aging process that affects many, if not most, individuals to some extent over time. Some are affected seriously, and some are affected much earlier than others. Sometimes these problems result from the onset of senility and Alzheimer's disease, whose symptoms may be very subtle and gradual. Over time, they will become painful and distressing to the victim, the victim's family, friends, neighbors, and eventually to the community association.

When this situation arises with a resident who has no support, it falls on the community association to deal with the resulting problems. In cases involving abusive or dangerous use of a unit or common areas by a resident, it may be necessary to seek injunctive relief for abatement of a nuisance. This would include harassing other residents, engaging in anti-social behavior, or destroying property. Do not overlook the possibility that the local law enforcement agencies should become involved in some cases.

Injunctive Relief

One remedy, which might be available through the statutes, or offered through the community association's governing documents, is to obtain a court order to force a disruptive resident to comply with the requirements of the documents. However, in the case of a resident who is not fully in control of his or her faculties, such a court order is unlikely to be effective.

Competency Hearings

As early as possible the association should attempt to locate a family member of the resident needing support. Make them aware of the situation, and—if they are unable to provide relief—ask them to petition the court for a competency hearing. It's always best to have a family member take this step in order to eliminate potential liability for the association; but, if necessary, the association can initiate the action itself if family members are unavailable or unwilling to help.

To seek a competency hearing, a parent, spouse, adult child, sibling, next of kin, or any three citizens must file a petition to the court. For associations, three board members would be appropriate. The individual in question is examined by two physicians and a layperson who report their findings to the judge. The court then determines whether the individual is incompetent and therefore in need of a court-appointed guardian.

This approach has been used successfully in Florida, Massachusetts, and New Jersey, among other states, for circumstances in which family cannot be located, to deal with aging residents who live alone in condominium units.

The advantage of this approach for the community association is that it will now have a competent legal guardian representing the resident in financial matters and who will be responsible for mitigating or controlling the resident's anti-social or unacceptable behavior.

Involuntary Intervention

Many jurisdictions in the country have laws that allow the state to intervene when a person becomes a hazard to himself, herself, or others. Hazard is generally defined as:

- deteriorated personal hygiene

- inappropriate or inadequate clothing when in public

- abusive, obscene, or inappropriate verbal interaction in response to ordinary conversation.

In Florida, for example, the Florida Mental Health Act—also known as the Baker Act—allows the state to involuntarily commit such a person for 72 hours of psychological evaluation and observation.

However, it further requires that some person swear out a statement concerning the action or behavior that is a danger, and sign that statement, before the state will take action. This isn't an action an association board would pursue except in the most extreme cases—when there's no family to contact or if the family withdraws its support and assistance—because of the risks involved.

These approaches have mixed results, but they may present viable options for extreme cases. However, it isn't likely that associations will rely on statutory solutions, as long as, for every act of involuntary assistance by the association—regardless of how well intentioned—there is the concomitant risk of liability for the association.

Weighing the Risks

There is always a potential for liability when anyone other than a family member files a petition for a competency hearing or commits a resident for evaluation. For example, there is the chance that the person, once released from involuntary custody, or a family member, will bring a lawsuit for false imprisonment or violation of civil rights. If a board member fears that a resident's children will bring legal action against him for trying to get mental health assistance or medical help for Mom or Dad, he will certainly think twice about getting involved.

Associations must balance these risks against the potential liability of *failing to act*. For example, another resident may sue the association if it fails to take action to protect association members from an abusive resident.

This is a viable concern, since courts around the country are increasingly holding community associations responsible for being their unit owners' keepers. They are delivering judgments against associations for failure to protect residents from crime, even when there has been no previous record of crime in the community. However unintended or innocent an Alzheimer's victim's actions, they may still constitute a crime against another resident.

In light of this trend toward accountability, and the possibility of its extension and expansion into the realm of aging issues and problems, association leaders should consider their actions carefully. Associations can achieve a comfortable level of assistance without incurring or assuming legal liability—and without becoming an "old age home"—by taking the following steps:

- Contact your local and state legislators. Encourage them to support and promote legislation that creates immunity for volunteers and relief from and limits on liability for those volunteers. Let them know that the association is attempting to provide assistance and support to residents who have neither family nor support networks outside the community.

- Educate volunteers. Be sure that board members or managers do not go into private dwellings just to see what is going on. Discourage volunteers from physically lifting residents, helping them with medication, and so on. Injuries and damage can occur to both the resident and the volunteer. Also, repairs and modifications to the interiors of dwellings should be made by someone who has the necessary expertise to do the work, and the necessary permits and licenses, when applicable.

- Create comprehensive policies and procedures for handling these issues. For example, require aggrieved neighbors to submit complaints in writing to the board or manager if they believe a resident is creating a nuisance, problem, or danger. If the danger is imminent, residents should be advised to call 911. Send notification of problems, not only to the offending resident, but to a family member, guardian, caregiver, or other "emergency contact" of record. If the resident is leasing, send a copy to the owner as well.

- Find out what services are available in the general community to assist the needy resident as well as the association.

- Work with the association's insurance professional to ensure that the Directors' and Officers' liability policies provide adequate coverage for the officers, directors, committee members, and other volunteers who are working with aging populations. If the likelihood of risk is high, consider upgrading the association's liability policy accordingly.

Inaccurate Self Image

Most people see themselves as much younger than their chronological age—it's just human nature. Seniors are no exception. They picture themselves as competent and capable, both mentally and physically, and in control of their lives. Baby Boomers in particular have a sense of competence and self-sufficiency. They're often not aware of the gradual deterioration in their health or of their mental and physical reflexes, which are the inevitable results of aging. For community associations with senior residents, an inaccurate self-concept can lead to serious trouble and possibly danger.

Consider the lady who clearly remembers her apartment in the city and how easy it was to walk for groceries and take care of her place 35 years ago. She believes she can still care for herself and her condominium unit. But, this same lady has a kitchen filled with bags of trash, and the remainder of her apartment is full of boxes of odds and ends collected over many years. There is barely a clear path from room to room, and the cockroaches have spread to the neighboring apartment. Or consider the gentleman who still dresses in a business suit every day, but has become incontinent.

In communities designed for seniors, monitoring and accommodating these types of problems are built into the system, just as playgrounds and kiddy pools are designed into communities for families with young children. But, all community associations—whether senior facilities or not—will be engulfed in a flood of seniors in the next few decades, and all will have to adjust to the new demographic landscape. Consider the challenges:

- **Board members and other volunteers may have diminished mental or physical capacities.**
  It's not unlikely that a community with a high percentage of retirees—who have time to volunteer—will find itself with a significant number of seniors on the board and on committees. If they exhibit the mental decline that sometimes comes with age, how will that affect the governance of the association? If a board member's physical capacity is limited due to age, what can the association do to accommodate full participation of an otherwise well qualified board member?

- **Seating viable board members may become increasingly difficult as the pool of capable candidates dwindles.**
  As the boards and residents age, communities become concerned about finding competent directors. One possible solution is for associations to consider hiring professional management services. Professional commu-

nity association management teams can take care of the day-to-day operations of the communities, and free the members for the more interesting pursuits of their lives and families. Perhaps paid professional board members are also in our futures.

- **Insurance premiums may become burdensome if residents cause damage.** Stories of absent-minded seniors leaving the gas on or the water running are common. Too many of these types of problems may threaten the association's insurance coverage—especially where water infiltration is involved.

- **Compliance with rules may be incomprehensible for some residents.** Community association rules baffle residents of all ages, but for those with failing eyesight, hearing loss, diminished mental capacity, or limited resources, compliance may be impossible. Being reasonable with elderly residents may require committing disproportionate human and financial resources, granting exemptions and variances, intervening benevolently, or subsidizing fines.

- **The needs of different demographic groups may conflict.** One of the natural outcomes of aging in place is that mixed demographic groups—seniors and families with small children—live side by side in the community. This is a positive and healthy arrangement for all involved, but it can put stress on the association when the very different needs of these groups come into conflict. Associations will need to find positive solutions that bring the community together while meeting individual needs.

Substance Abuse

An estimated 10 percent of the 43 million older adults in the U.S. are addicted to alcohol or prescription medication. In addition, abuse of over-the-counter drugs is a serious problem among the older population.

It's a costly problem. In 1998, a study conducted at the National Center on Addiction and Substance Abuse at Columbia University found that the treatment cost for elderly addiction was more than $30 billion just for women. Since older adults are the fastest growing segment of the population in the U.S., the costs are going to increase in the future. By 2018, the costs of alcohol- and drug-related inpatient hospital bills, nursing home bills, physician services, and home health care are expected to approach $100 billion.

Compounding the problem is the fact that the symptoms of aging and of substance abuse are very similar—memory loss, paralysis, blindness, dementia, depression, insomnia, and malnutrition. Caretakers, neighbors, and even doctors sometimes fail to recognize alcohol and drug abuse among the elderly. Fortunately, the number of doctors and clinics specializing in the medical problems of the older citizen is increasing, as are alcohol and drug abuse treatment centers aimed exclusively at senior citizens.

The physical challenges associated with drug and alcohol abuse are very real problems—not just for the elderly, but for their community associations as well. Retirees who were once able to control their drinking because they had appointments to keep, people to see, and reasons to get dressed in the morning, now drink for something to do to fill their time.

As we grow older, it takes less alcohol to drastically impair function. So, the healthy, active, and responsible Baby Boomer—who otherwise doesn't overindulge—may be affected nonetheless.

The problems resulting for community associations can be challenging—particularly when board members are affected. Senior residents with impaired judgment, erratic behavior, and altered personalities are less likely to comply with rules, pay assessments on time, or be good neighbors.

What can associations do to mitigate this problem? Unfortunately, substance abuse is a national epidemic. Community associations probably can't do much more than what countless other groups are already doing; but they needn't duplicate those efforts, either. Take advantage of the numerous drug and alcohol treatment options available through the state and local governments. Make family members aware of problems or potential problems. Intervene directly if necessary—but only *after* the association attorney has been contacted—and use the help of professionals, including police and government agencies.

Costs

However we look at it, and beyond the issues of retrofitting current facilities, there are significant daily costs which can be associated with meeting the challenges presented by aging residents in community associations.

These costs are often indirect or hidden costs that may not show up as a line in the budget, but which will consume resources—particularly, human resources. These are the everyday costs of operations, including the community association manager's time, maintenance personnel, clerical support staff, and others who will work to meet the disproportionate needs of the aging individuals, over and above the needs of the community at large.

Depending on the demands, additional staff or more volunteers may be needed to keep up with these needs, which may result in a line in the budget after all. Some direct costs may accumulate such as commercial parking for employees so that an elderly resident can be granted reserved handicapped parking.

Financial Realities

Many people embarking on retirement are not financially prepared. In 2001, nine percent of Americans ages 65 to 74 lived in poverty. For those ages 75 to 84, the number increases to 10 percent. And for those 85 and older, the number leaps to 14 percent living in poverty in the U.S. The majority of these are single women.

This may be the result of inadequate income, catastrophic illness, death of a spouse, lack of professional assistance or good advice, or they have simply outlived their savings. Many have seen their retirement funds dwindle alarmingly in a volatile stock market. Social Security, which was originally designed to support a retired person or a surviving spouse for four or five years, is now stretched to provide support for 15 to 20 years after retirement.

Future retirees are seeing their resources prematurely drained by too many dependents. This is the Sandwich Generation—people in their 40's and 50's who, because they started their own families later in life, are now supporting their own children *and* their aging or infirm parents, who may or may not reside with them.

Today's financial limitations and longer life spans are also resulting in the old caring for the older. In one case, a woman who was 103 years old moved in with her 66-year-old daughter and the daughter's husband. The daughter is now sharing her financial resources with her mother instead of preparing for her own retirement; and she's spending her physical resources on her mother instead of focusing on her own health issues, which can be significant. This is not an isolated case. According to the U.S. Bureau of the Census, 20 percent of all homes were headed by a person aged 65 or over in 2002, and the percent will increase by 2010.

The emotional, physical, and financial strain can be immensely stressful to those who are entering their own retirement years. Unfortunately, some people can't cope. They strand their elders in condominium units or, worse, discard them altogether. A recent newspaper story reported on an elderly woman who was found alone in a bus station, far from home. A note pinned to her jacket explained that her family could not care for her, and they hoped some kind stranger would take her in.

Undoubtedly all these factors will have an impact on senior residents' ability to pay assessments to the community association, and community associations will need to adjust to these realities. Financial creativity, innovation, and even sacrifice may be needed. For example:

- Associations may have to make arrangements for family members to pay a relative's assessments. Association bookkeeping and billing procedures may need to accommodate payment plans in which multiple family members subsidize a financially limited parent.

- Assessments might be substantially affected by a resident's ability to pay. In 2002, one quarter of all people over 65 living alone had no children, and this figure isn't expected to change before 2020. Associations may find there are no family members to turn to for help with a senior resident in the community.

- Occupancy restrictions may become archaic considerations. A survey published in the *Miami Herald* in 1995 showed that unmarried couples over the age of 45 were the fastest growing type of household in Florida and across the nation. Singles were moving in together for mutual emotional support, health care, and social company, as well as to pool finances for a better quality of life. No projections are available for how this trend might continue in the future, but if it follows the other trends projected by the Census Bureau, it will increase. In fact, this consolidation of resources may extend beyond traditional "couples" to include the roommate paradigm where several seniors share a home—a la "The Golden Girls."

None of these issues are new to community associations; however, when they affect or involve an aging population, they take on new dimensions that challenge association leaders to envision entirely new paradigms, new approaches, and new solutions. These shouldn't be insurmountable. Recognizing the situation, and working on those new approaches now will help associations prepare for what's ahead.

Furthermore, this cloud has its silver lining: others are starting to prepare and much of what needs to be done is already known. In addition, many of the retiring Baby Boomers will become Baby Zoomers—Baby Boomers who see retirement as the fast lane to a more energetic, new life characterized by healthy living, a high level of physical activity, and a quest for further education, and who possess technological and financial savvy. The Yuppie Elderly will be better educated and enjoy better health than any prior generation of retirees. They will be assets to their associations—offsetting some of the liabilities and mitigating some of the challenges.

CHAPTER 2

Silver Linings

The parents of the Baby Boomers, who lived through the Great Depression, saw home ownership as the ultimate mark of success. Boomers absorbed this value as children, so, understandably, those who have now reached a level of economic success want to recapture the quality of life they grew up with.

In the 1960's, Americans looked for "the house." In the 1970's, the subdivision and the master plan were important. In the 1980's and 1990's, lifestyle was the commodity. But, now, in the 21st century, as the Baby Boomers burgeon into the largest home-buying demographic, "community" is coming into it's own once again. Boomers are looking for an interesting and convenient place to live, with the possibility of becoming involved in the community. They don't want to cocoon; they want to congregate. They're looking for an "old-fangled new town." In order to achieve this, there must be an "architecture of engagement" inherent in designing a platform from which a new kind of community will grow.

Fortunately, architects and planners are becoming involved in and committed to just such an approach—called traditional neighborhood development. Traditional neighborhoods are mixed-use communities; that is, within the residential areas, developers include commercial sites like grocery stores, drugstores, dry cleaners, and recreational facilities.

All over the country, developers are constructing these pedestrian friendly communities so residents have pedestrian access to amenities, thus eliminating the need for a vehicle. People who do not drive, or who don't wish to drive, still have access to basic services, activities, and recreation—conveniently close to home. This is good news for seniors especially.

Traditional neighborhoods also have a variety of home styles that provide choices in price and design that adds visual interest. In some communities, large single-family homes are mixed with smaller townhouses and condominiums—not only in the same neighborhood, but even on the same block. The result is a mix of ages, life stages, and incomes in the same area.

Not only are the neighborhoods themselves evolving into more livable places for seniors, but the homes within them are being designed to accommodate residents through progressive life stages.

Savvy developers are building two-story homes with stacking closets, one above the other, to allow for future installation of a small elevator—if needed—to enable easy access to all levels of the home. In fact, some new homes, admittedly in the higher price ranges, are being built with elevators already installed. Designers are making floor plans available in which all living space is contained on a single floor. And, they're designing and building two-story houses with master bedroom suites on the ground floor so that residents can live comfortably on the first level, should that become necessary later because of declining health or advancing age.

Other design elements that incorporate a life-span concept include:

- Sinks and doors use levers instead of knobs.

- Doorways and halls are wide enough to allow wheelchair access.

- Exits to the outdoors have gradual sloping paths, rather than steps.

- Showers have pull down seats.

- Walls are reinforced to support grab bars.

- Ovens open from the side to eliminate reaching over a hot door.

Technology

Community associations are beginning to use the Internet to create a global front porch. Many have created community websites, from which residents can access the schedule of events, minutes of board meetings, financial reports, association documents, information about the community, chat rooms, and bulletin boards.

Seniors Are Wired

Not surprisingly, seniors are logging on to the Internet in record numbers. People over the age of 50 comprise the fastest growing population of Internet users—probably reflecting the increasing number of Baby Boomers who are crossing into the 55+ category. The oldest Baby Boomers' careers paralleled the emergence of technology in the work place. The youngest Boomers have never experienced a work environment *without* technology. Even if not entirely computer savvy, neither are Boomers computer phobic. They can be expected not only to keep up with technology as they age further, but to demand innovative electronic and wireless services in their homes as they age.

Even seniors who did not have careers that accustomed them to the benefits of computer technology are realizing the need to learn and use it. Introductory courses in computer use and Internet access are filled to capacity at local colleges. SeniorNet, a paid membership website encourages seniors to use the Internet to enrich their lives. And, recognizing that people over the age of 55 still have feelings and interest in relationships, numerous online dating services have sections specifically for seniors or for those simply looking for a golf partner or other platonic companionship. For example, America Online hosts a web-based match-making section, which gives seniors an opportunity to meet. AOL estimates that its services have sparked as many as 10,000 marriages over the years, many of these among the elderly.

Online Voting and Net Meetings

The convergence of technology, federal regulation, and the dramatic increase in the number of seniors living in community associations may soon bring about a change in standard association procedures. For example, some associations are already taking advantage of electronic signature laws to encourage residents to vote online and assign proxies via e-mail. Not only does this allow homebound residents, such as seniors, to participate in the association's democratic process, it increases participation among all residents because of its convenience. The day is not far off when residents will have the opportunity to attend a community association membership meeting via the net, and maybe the meeting will be held entirely on the net, rather than in a meeting room.

Home-Based Businesses

Technology will play a major role in the second careers of Baby Boomers who will continue to work from their homes after retirement.

What will that mean for the growth of home-based businesses? With the boom in technological development, futurists predict that more than half of the work force will be working out of their homes, using their computer systems and taking advantage of Internet business possibilities. Thus, with the development of technology, we will see a new definition or even disappearance of retirement as we have known it. Community associations will need to revisit the rationale behind the prohibitions against home-based business.

Education

According to the U.S. Census Bureau's Current Population Survey conducted in 2002, between 1950 and 2002, the number of Americans over age 65 who had earned at least a bachelor's degree increased from just under four percent to almost 17 percent.

In 2002, 35 percent of people over age 65 did not have high school diplomas. In 2010, 25 percent of Americans over 65 will not have finished high school. And, by 2020, that number will drop to 12 percent. While these are very positive improvements, seniors nevertheless are the least educated demographic in America. Furthermore, the Population Survey found that education level does not translate into improved English skills—particularly among minorities.

Homeowner Education

An increasing number of seniors will be living in community associations in the coming decades, and many of them will be serving on their association's boards and committees. Therefore, education of boards, volunteers, and residents is critical. Associations must ensure that volunteers who are directors or participating on committees are well trained—not only about association governance responsibilities, but also about the special needs of senior residents.

Manager Education

As the number of seniors in community associations mushrooms over the next 20 years, professional community managers will find themselves dealing more and more often with problems perhaps only occasionally encountered today. Proper training will be needed for them to do their jobs effectively. This includes training staff, service personnel, on-site managers, and even office staff. A basic understanding of "elder issues" will become essential. For example:

- What are the signs of substance abuse and diminished capacity? How should managers deal with these conditions?

- What do federal and state regulations require with regard to fair housing, fair debt collection, or Americans with disabilities, and how do these laws affect seniors?

- What is strategic planning, and how does a community association form a long-term plan for meeting the needs of its elderly population?

- How does an association go about changing its governing documents in order to accommodate the needs of aging residents?

- How do already overworked managers meet the disproportionate demands of older residents?

Transportation

With the ever-increasing number of drivers over age 55, municipalities and counties, highway engineers, safety groups, and automobile manufacturers will inevitably make changes to roads and vehicles to accommodate these drivers' diminished visual and hearing acuity and slowing reflexes. Community associations should also take these factors into consideration as a regular aspect of maintenance. For example, associations can make the following changes or improvements:

- Make street signs larger than local standards require. Ensure they are brightly lit, well placed, and easy to read.

- Place traffic control signs farther in advance; and place notifications ahead of them. For example, "Stop Ahead" might be appropriate several hundred feet before the actual "Stop" sign.

- Increase common area street and parking area lighting.

- Use plenty of pavement markings on community streets and parking lots.

- Ensure that pavement markers and signs are highly reflective and that they maintain their reflective properties when wet.

Eventually Baby Boomers will reach an age when they can no longer drive. When that time comes, a record number of people will need alternate forms of transportation. Improvements to public transportation will be required, if these seniors who no longer drive are to have a viable alternative. But until that happens, there are things associations can do to meet the transportation needs of their residents who do not drive.

- Work with local transportation authorities to schedule a regular bus stop within the community.

- Augment public transportation with community association sponsored shuttle service to local public transportation hubs.

- Contact local taxi companies to negotiate reduced rates for residents on fixed incomes for transportation to health care facilities. Offer free advertising in the association newsletter in exchange.

- Organize a car pool or committee that will coordinate rides to doctors, recreational activities, and family gatherings.

- Check with state and local social services agencies, some of which provide transportation services that will pick up seniors and drive them to shopping malls, beauty salons, and doctor's offices.

Strategic Planning

Preparing a community for the inevitable changes that the aging Baby Boomers will bring about in the next several decades is a large undertaking—perhaps even overwhelming considering all the implications. One effective way to embark is with strategic planning.

The strategic planning process begins with a mission statement. Every community association should develop a mission statement; this focuses energy and thought on identifying goals and developing strategies for achieving them. Boards, committees, professional management, support staff, the community association attorney, and the residents should work together to develop the mission statement, in order to create a definition of the community culture, and to create a sense of commonality among all who are involved in the community as a whole.

Part of the strategic planning process will involve setting goals. It's worthwhile to set short- and long-term goals for the operation, improvement, and development of the community's plan for meeting the needs of an aging population.

Strategic planning is a formal process with numerous steps; it requires more explanation than is possible within the scope of this text. It's a very effective process for preparing for the future, and community associations are encouraged to learn more about it and make use of it.

Municipal Services Delivery

Associations should work closely with their local municipalities to encourage them to review their services and make changes to accommodate individuals who are now staying in their pre-retirement homes. Associations should also work with local providers of goods and services to meet the needs of residents with limited mobility.

For example, many large grocery stores are beginning to make home deliveries again, as they did early in the last century. In almost all instances, orders can be placed via the Internet. Veterinarians, recognizing the limitations of their elderly clients, are making house calls. Mobile animal hospital vans are becoming a common sight in urban areas. In many areas, dry cleaners are making deliveries as well. Services that were originally intended to accommodate busy professionals are now increasingly meeting the needs of residents who do not drive or who are home bound—often seniors.

Associations can help facilitate these types of services for their residents by negotiating senior or group discounts with local retailers, providing a central pick-up or drop-off location, placing orders online for seniors who don't have Internet access, or simply making residents aware of what's available in the community by publishing relevant information in the association newsletter or listing it on the association website.

Making Modifications and Providing Services

Traditional retirement communities include built-in support systems for some degree of assisted living. However, all community associations can take steps to assist older residents without turning themselves into "retirement communities." The recommendations in this section, while intended to make life easier for associations with aging populations, will benefit *all* residents regardless of age.

Boards can modernize and up-grade landscaping, grounds, and common areas to make the community amenities accessible to those who are physically challenged by age or infirmity. In some cases, this may require approval by the members or amendments to the governing documents, but the return on the investment in effort is worthwhile and contributes significantly to the quality of life for everyone.

Requiring equally as much effort as making modifications is providing services; however, there are numerous no-cost and low-cost steps associations can take to facilitate access to services and to directly provide services to residents that will make the community a comfortable place for seniors.

No-Cost or Low-Cost Common Area Modifications That Aid Seniors

- Place decals on the windows of residents who want to be easily identified in case of emergency.

- Apply no-slip or non-skid coatings to surfaces like sidewalks, catwalks, ramps, and other common areas that might pose a challenge for people with limited mobility. Watch for potentially slippery surfaces—like linoleum or tile—especially if there's a possibility that the surface will get wet.

- Install extra lighting and increase the output of existing lighting. Audit indoor and outdoor lighting to identify weakly illuminated areas. Bear in mind the special limitations of seniors who may have impaired or limited vision.

- Install ramps and handrails at building entrances.

- Create or add additional curb cuts.

- Wire units for in-house communications, or provide a panic button or intercom that allows residents with special needs to alert a central monitoring station when they need help. The association doesn't necessarily have to pay for these modifications, or require them in every home. But it can research vendors and options, coordinate a monitoring station, and make residents aware that the services are available if they're interested and willing to pay for them.

- Mount signal lights at the front of buildings, in a multi-building community, to aid emergency vehicles in locating a particular residence.

- Evaluate landscaping with an eye toward unobstructed access. Remove or trim any vegetation that might impede pedestrians who use canes, walkers, or wheel chairs. Also look for and correct landscaping features that interfere with lighting.

- Inspect concrete and asphalt surfaces, and repair any potential trip hazards.

- Affix reflective tape on multi-level surfaces such as steps and curbs. Affix reflectors to handrails, gates, and other items that may be difficult to locate in low light.

No-Cost or Low-Cost Community Association Services That Aid Seniors

- Develop a program for orienting and welcoming new residents to the association. This will help eliminate the isolation most seniors—especially those who are alone—experience when they move into a new environment. Help them meet their neighbors, and find out who they are. Use their skills and interests to get them involved in the community.

- Provide local authorities (EMTs, fire and rescue) with the names and addresses of high-risk residents. Notify them of the signal light or window decal system used by the community association.

- Negotiate with vendors for group rates for retrofitting home interiors. Provide the list of vendors and the price list to residents who may wish to have grab bars installed or have other modifications made within their homes.

- Research and make available to residents information on federal, state, and local social service agencies. Check the local yellow pages or county website. Contact appropriate agencies, and discuss with them how the association can work with them to coordinate the delivery of services to seniors. For example, Meals on Wheels, home nursing visits, support groups for spouses and family of Alzheimer's disease patients, traveling blood pressure, vision, and hearing testing, and many other services are available. (For a brief list of national resource organizations, see Appendix 4.)

- Contact the state Division of Aging or Long Term Care (LTC) Ombudsman, which coordinates the flow of information and resolves problems as they arise. The scope of assistance and communication varies widely from state to state, but the association should at least familiarize itself with what's available and take full advantage of all services. (See Appendix 2.)

- Determine whether your local community has an adult day care center. This industry is emerging in response to market need. These centers provide supervised activities, assistance, lunches, and sometimes transportation. Many such centers are connected with social services.

- Talk to the professionals who work for the community association. Encourage them to work with state and federal legislators, local businesses, and health care providers to familiarize them with the issues of aging in place and the needs of an aging population so that creative solutions and services can be ready when they're needed.

- Create a committee to organize association-sponsored seniors programs such as social events, educational programs, crafts events, and travel opportunities. Many such programs can be arranged through outside groups. Through active lifestyles, the quality of aging is vastly improved.

- Arrange for seniors to have opportunities for exercise such as balance training, aerobics, and strength training either on the association premises or at a local senior center. Ongoing research shows that exercise and proper nutrition are very beneficial for older persons.

- Work with local agencies to facilitate counseling for residents, including middle-aged residents, senior citizens, and their families. Encourage them to plan well in advance for the inevitable decline that comes with aging. Planning should also address financial security and health care needs.

- Maintain detailed records about senior residents, including whether they have a live-in caregiver; name, address, telephone number of next of kin or emergency contact; name and telephone number of general medical practitioner; a list of medical conditions and medications; use of a hearing aid, cane, wheelchair, or glasses. (See Appendix 5 for a sample form for collecting this information.)

Change the Governing Documents

The day is not far off when existing associations will need to amend their governing documents, and new associations will need to draft original documents, in ways that address the issues resulting from an increasing number of residents who are aging in place. This will require a basic paradigm shift for community association leaders in order to correct the imbalance—which currently tips toward protecting property more than valuing people. Some of these issues include:

Right of Access

In Florida, the statutes and many governing documents of condominium communities guarantee an irrevocable right of access to a unit in order to:

- protect other units

- repair or maintain the common elements

- gain access to units from which noxious odors are emanating

- make arrangements for cleanup and pest control

    It further gives the association the right to:

- enter for repair and maintenance, including pest control and clean-up within a dwelling unit

- assess for the expenses of such maintenance and repair

- place a lien against the dwelling unit to collect expenses of maintenance and repair

    The right of access is a business necessity when working with any resident, but it becomes especially important when dealing with residents whose capability, mobility, or reasoning may be impaired due to the effects of age. Indeed, it amounts to protection provided by the association to senior residents.

    Florida is just one example. Other states are following suit, and community association industry professionals should continue to push for these rights in state statutes and governing documents for all types of covenant controlled communities.

Require Emergency Medical Data

The first line of defense in an emergency is ready access to meaningful information. Association directors can adopt rules and regulations requiring that the association maintain medical and other personal records on each resident. However, writing new governing documents or changing existing ones requiring this information strengthens the associations position in collecting and maintaining it.

Naturally residents will be reluctant to provide it; however, it will protect the association and the resident—particularly an aging resident or a resident with few resources. Information that should be required according to the governing documents includes:

- name, age, blood type

- next of kin, including name, address, phone, and relationship

- emergency telephone contact (This should be a family member or someone who can act with authority on behalf of the resident—preferably with power of attorney.)

- medical conditions

- medications taken or special equipment used

- physician's name, address, and phone number

Assure residents that this information will be kept confidential, and it will only be used if there's an emergency. Keep these records up-to-date, and periodically remind residents to provide new information. While this is a bookkeeping imposition, ultimately, it can save the association a great deal of time and energy, and possibly save the life of a resident.

See Appendix 5 for a sample emergency medical information form currently being used with success by several community associations.

Relax Occupancy Requirements

More seniors with fewer resources, fewer places to go, and fewer support systems will soon change the character of "family" as most have known it. It will be necessary to relax certain restrictions in governing documents and local statutes in order to accommodate the needs of the burgeoning senior cohort in our communities over the next few years. For example:

- With an increasing number of people caring for elderly parents and raising families at the same time, "single family" may be redefined to include parents and children of residents as authorized occupants.

- Density restrictions can be structured to accommodate living arrangements that become necessary because of financial need or health problems.

- Prohibitions against "renters" or subletting should be subject to exceptions for health care providers and live-in caregivers.

Provide Appropriate Authority

Governing documents generally give boards rule-making authority, the ability to regulate activities, and to allocate funds as they see fit. However, language that specifically empowers the board to act on behalf of the association and the community for issues related to aging in place will strengthen the association's ability to meet the needs of aging residents. For example, governing documents could empower boards to:

- spend money if required for services or physical plant modifications to reasonably accommodate an aging population

- pursue enforcement

- hire a professional social services agent as an employee of the association

- exchange parking spaces to accommodate physical incapacity

Review the governing documents with an eye toward the current culture of the community, and make changes in the restrictions if they are warranted. Of course, changing governing documents is a complex undertaking best approached in close consultation with the association attorney.

It's possible that your association is ahead of this curve and already has the authority to undertake many of the necessary steps to accommodate its aging population. If you're unsure, check with the association attorney to determine the association's authority to act.

CHAPTER 3

Conclusion

W e're all familiar with the ongoing debate about the future of Social Security and whether it will be able to support the tremendous increase of beneficiaries when the Baby Boomers begin to retire. The outcome of this debate has sobering implications for community associations. The projections are undeniable: more retirees will stay in their pre-retirement homes longer, have fewer family members to support them, and receive diminishing Social Security benefits. Communities will inevitably find themselves filling gaps in the overall well being of their senior residents.

Baby Boomers will begin retiring in a few short years. Now is the time for community associations to begin thinking about and planning for integrating their needs into the daily routine of association business.

Begin with small steps, and work toward a paradigm shift in the approach the association takes toward its various activities. For example, many of the recommendations in this book are suitable for all ages, and emerge from a common-sense approach to being part of a community. But for those in the community who are aging, the recommendations take on a greater meaning—from little extras to big essentials. For example, this book recommends that associations reach out to new residents to welcome them to the community—common advice, often heard. A young family with small children may be delighted by a welcoming visit, but they're active and busy and might not think twice if they *didn't* get such a visit. On the other hand, a welcoming visit from a board member or community resident to a recently widowed senior would probably make a significant difference in the quality of that person's community living experience.

Awareness of these types of differences is the first step. Associations should move on to the other steps outlined in this book in order to begin their preparations for successfully living with those who will age in the place where they are right now—your association.

References

U.S. Census Bureau, Current Population Survey Reports, "Marital Status and Living Arrangements," March 2000.

Federal Interagency Forum on Aging Related Statistics, "Older Americans 2000: Key Indicators of Well-Being." (U.S. Census Bureau, Current Population Survey, Annual Social and Economic Supplement, 2002.)

Jacob Siegel, "Aging into the 21st Century," National Aging Information Center, Administration on Aging, U.S. Department of Health and Human Services, 1996.

Kunkel, S.R., & Applebaum, R.A. (1992). Estimating the Prevalence of Long-Term Disability for An Aging Society. *Journal of Gerontology: Social Sciences*, 475, S253-S260.

U.S. National Center for Health Statistics (1996). Interagency Forum on Aging Related Statistics; and University of Illinois at Chicago, School of Public Health, and University of Chicago, "Projections of Health Status and Use of Health Care of Older Americans" (Occasional Paper from the National Center for Health Statistics, Centers for Disease Control and Prevention).

Appendix 1—The Community Association of the Future

Community associations come in all shapes, sizes, heights, and configurations, and may include condominiums, condominium hotels and cruise ships, timeshares, cooperatives, homeowner and property owner associations, master associations, dockominiums, manufactured housing parks, and any combination of these. No matter what form they take, all common interest communities share certain characteristics that create the same circumstances for those who live in them.

- All community associations have a set of governing documents. While they may differ in their particulars from one association to the next, these documents create obligations and responsibilities for owners, through the use of covenants and restrictions.

- All community associations have "members." Membership is mandatory and automatic when buyers take title to their lots or units.

- All community associations require members to pay assessments. Assessments, or dues, pay for maintaining, repairing, and replacing common property and for daily operations.

- All community association members have an undivided ownership interest in the property.

Community Associations in the 20th Century

In the United States, condominiums, cooperatives, and planned communities have evolved in phases over the last 150 years. Planned communities were first developed in the 1820's, cooperatives arrived from Europe around 1900, and condominiums increased noticeably after 1961 when the federal housing law was modified.

Early in the 20th century, improved transportation and an abundance of land and resources gave rise to the first suburbs, which were developed around the major cities on the east coast of the United States, following the streetcar lines.

By the mid-1950's, the development of the interstate highway system and the exploding automobile market, turned Americans into a mobile population following jobs and family all over the country. The newly mobile could also easily commute downtown—or anywhere—to work, which guaranteed the growth of suburbia. Eventually, inner cities became home largely to those who could not afford to own their homes or cars, while the suburbs expanded at alarming rates.

Urban Sprawl

The inevitable result of the unabated burgeoning of suburbia has been urban sprawl, which occurs when *something* gets built on every tract of available land—without regard for environmental impact, aesthetic issues, or the ability of local governments to provide utilities, transportation, education, or recreation.

Suburbia began as a pattern of widespread, low-density residential and commercial settlements in which developers leap-frogged around and beyond already established communities without regard for design or function.

At the time, this wasn't perceived as a problem because the automobile allowed people to move around easily from one place to another. In fact, it increased Americans' dependence on automobiles and decreased the need for public transportation. Furthermore, suburbia continued to expand because the automobile allowed workers to commute ever farther between home and work. Ironically, there has been a terrible impact on the human condition as a result of those long commutes from home to work, and too many hours spent in the car, including the emergence of "road rage" as a commonly recognized psychological disorder.

The unchecked advance of suburbia—little or no centralized planning or control of land use, widespread strip commercial development, segregation of specialized types of land uses in separate zones, and very little planning for low income housing—has inevitably transformed the suburbs from a once-idyllic dream destination into today's urban sprawl.

Municipalities and developers have now discovered there is a huge cost to maintain this far-flung infrastructure. Furthermore, urban sprawl has negatively impacted the environment and led to deteriorating infrastructures that cause public danger and health hazards.

The result has been a marked diminishing of the quality of life for millions of Americans caused by traffic congestion and long commutes, air pollution, squandered energy resources, escalating costs of living, lack of affordable housing, and an increasing feeling of personal isolation.

Few politicians seem willing to do much about this problem because of the "nimtoo" creed—Not In My Term Of Office—shorthand for a reluctance to endorse change or espouse a potentially unpopular point of view, particularly in an election year.

Community Associations in the 21st Century

It's no wonder that—at a time when suburbia was strained to the limits by urban sprawl, inner cities were deteriorating, and ever-denser populations burdened municipal infrastructures everywhere—community associations emerged as a highly viable housing system for a large segment of America. Thus, by 2000, there were approximately 215,000 community associations in the United States, comprising 18 million housing units and approximately 42 million residents—based on best estimates. More than half the states required developers to create associations for their new housing projects. Furthermore, many inner-city restoration projects were reclaiming neighborhoods and creating community associations where none existed before.

Nevertheless, the very factors that make community associations attractive—a weak economy and the burdens of urban sprawl—also significantly challenge them. These factors affect associations in more ways than might be expected and for many reasons. Governing documents *require* boards to maintain property values through upkeep, insure the association and its representatives, fund reserves, and meet expenses. Meeting these fiduciary obligations can be extremely difficult when the economy is lagging and association budgets have to subsidize municipal services. And that's just the beginning.

Increased Maintenance and Repair Costs

Today, the structural components of many buildings are aging. The construction boom that followed WWII carried over as far as the 1960's and 1970's. Many of these older buildings have become today's community associations through conversions and other means. They require constant maintenance. Even associations built recently can require constant maintenance because they exist in climates where salt air or desert sun punish the common elements relentlessly, or because building codes have relaxed in order to accommodate an evolving construction industry. The reality is that for all associations—regardless of the age of the property—maintaining and repairing the common elements and common areas is a costly proposition.

Increased Insurance Costs

The insurance market is global, and even without losses in the immediate geographic vicinity, a community association may face occasional large increases in premiums, sometimes as high as 100 percent from one year to the next. Not only do natural disasters like hurricanes and other storms, floods, fires, and so on, increase the costs of insurance, but previously unheard of problems—like toxic mold—are now rendering some associations virtually uninsurable. Without insurance, these associations have to reserve cash to cover the expenses they might face due to loss or liability. Furthermore, associations face liability issues today that were unimagined a decade ago—such as sexual harassment and employment discrimination—against which they must insure themselves.

Increased Reserve Costs

At no time do boards struggle more with the idea of whether to have fully-funded reserve accounts than when the economy is weak and just meeting expenses is a challenge. Trying to educate members about the need for funding reserves and for long-range planning regarding maintenance and repair of the common property is as big a struggle.

Embattled Boards

Boards of community associations often find themselves faced with difficult decisions on how to cover these costs. Sometime they must levy large special assessments or increase monthly assessments, sometimes in the face of membership opposition and open resistance. Faced with such opposition, many board members are reluctant to increase assessments during their terms to avoid becoming the target of owner attacks.

Consequently, boards are choosing alternative methods of financing repair and reconstruction projects, funding reserves, and meeting insurance requirements. These bring with them some difficult decisions, and sometimes reluctance from the members.

This is particularly challenging among retirement-age populations, who reason that they won't be there when the roof needs to be replaced.

Legislative Complications

Community associations today are subject to legislation at the federal, state, and local levels—all governing their operations. The list can be staggering: the Fair Housing Act, the Telecommunications Act, and bankruptcy and fair credit collection laws. In addition to condominium, cooperative, timeshare, mobile home, homeowners association, and corporate laws, associations are also subject to fire safety laws, zoning ordinances, and on and on.

After all that, associations are also subject to their governing documents which—if they were written in the community-association-booming 1960's or 1970's, as many were—may be neither adequate nor even legal and proper for running today's community associations, given the extensive lifestyle and legislative changes that have evolved since those times. Yet, boards are continuing to struggle to comply with and enforce these outmoded documents. For example, documents written before 1975 (when there were no sport utility vehicles) commonly prohibited trucks and vans. In 2003, 40 percent of the vehicles on the road fall in the SUV or RV category.

Compliance Issues

Current community-association governance models are based on absolutes and generalizations, which arise out of an inability to agree on a vision for the community and results in a perception that the members have no input in the governance of their homes. Feelings of disassociation lead to violations of the governing documents, which in turn lead to extreme measures, like litigation, on the part of the associations to promote compliance. But, Ambrose Bierce once described litigation as "a machine you go into as a pig and come out as a sausage." Sometimes, it seems as if litigation is part of the problem, rather than the best solution.

Well-meaning but misguided boards working from outdated documents have, unfortunately, moved some associations away from the model of participatory democracy—to the detriment of the community association concept and to the delight of the public press.

Effects on Aging Residents

These challenges are significant for managers and boards of community associations. But their effect on senior residents can be particularly problematic. Residents on fixed incomes may find it burdensome to pay assessments—especially special assessments. Physical or mental limitations may make it difficult for seniors to comply with rules. The demand for reserved handicapped parking may exceed the association's available space. The list goes on and on.

Nevertheless, community associations of the 21st century will overcome these challenges—they will have to, one way or another.

Appendix 2—Agencies on Aging and Long Term Care Ombudsman

Long Term Care Ombudsman programs investigate and resolve complaints of elder abuse made by or for individual residents in long-term care facilities. Ombudsman programs advocate for residents in the long-term care system through public education and consensus building. In addition, these programs address concerns about quality of care or financial abuse; suspected physical, mental, or emotional abuse of residents; and provide qualified personnel to attend resident care planning and family council meetings.

National Resource

National Long Term Care Ombudsman Resource Center
1424 16th Street, NW, Ste 202
Washington, D.C. 20036
Phone: 202-332-2275
Fax: 202-332-2949
E-mail: ombudcenter@nccnhr.org
Website:
www.ltcombudsman.org/default.cfm

State Agencies

Alabama
Alabama Dept. of Senior Services
770 Washington Ave., RSA Plaza Ste. 470
Montgomery, AL 36130
Phone: 334-242-5743
Fax: 334-242-5594
Email: ageline@adss.state.al.us
Website: www.adss.state.al.us

LTC Ombudsman: Same as above.

Alaska
Office location:
Alaska Commission on Aging
State Office Bldg, Rm 757, 7th Fl.
333 West Willoughby Ave.
Juneau, Alaska
Phone: 907-465-4879
Website: www.alaskaaging.org

Mailing address:
Alaska Commission on Aging
Alaska Dept of Health & Social Services

PO Box 110693
Juneau, AK 99811-0693

LTC Ombudsman
Alaska Mental Health Trust Authority
Office of the State LTC Ombudsman
550 West 7th Ave., Ste. 1830
Anchorage, AK 99501
Phone: 907-334-4480
Fax: 907-334-4486
Website: www.mhtrust.org

Arizona
Aging & Adult Administration
1789 W. Jefferson, Site Code 950A
Phoenix, AZ 85007
Phone: 602-542-4446
Fax: 602-542-6575
E-mail: askdesaaa@mail.de.state.az.us
Website: www.de.state.az.us/aaa

LTC Ombudsman
Arizona Aging & Adult Administration
1789 West Jefferson, 2SW 950A
Phoenix, AZ 85007
Phone: 602-542-6454
Fax: 602-542-6575
Website: www.de.state.az.us/aaa/
programs/ombudsman/default.asp

Arkansas
Div. of Aging & Adult Services
Arkansas Dept. of Human Services
7th & Main St.
P.O. Box 1437, Slot S-530
Little Rock, AR 72203
Phone: 501-682-2441

Fax: 501-682-8155
Website: www.state.ar.us/dhs/aging/
Also, www.carescout.com/state_ar_little-rock.htm contains a list of resources in Arkansas for older citizens.

LTC Ombudsman
Address & phone same as above.
Website: www.arombudsman.com

California
California Dept. of Aging
1600 K St.
Sacramento, CA 95814
Phone: 916-322-3887
FAX: 916-324-4989
TTY 1-800-735-2929
Website: www.aging.state.ca.us/index.html

LTC Ombudsman
Address & phone same as above.
Website: www.aging.state.ca.us/html/
programs/ombudsman.html

Colorado
Colorado Dept. of Social Services
Div. of Aging & Adult Services
1575 Sherman St., 10th Floor
Denver, CO 80203
Phone: 303-866-2800
Fax: 303-866-2696
Website:
www.cdhs.state.co.us/oss/aas/index1.html

LTC Ombudsman
The Legal Center
455 Sherman St., Ste. 130
Denver, CO 80203
Phone: 1-800-288-1376
Fax: 303-722-0720
Website: www.thelegalcenter.org/
services_older.html

Connecticut
Connecticut Dept. of Social Services
Elderly Services Div.
25 Sigourney St., 10th Floor
Hartford, CT 06106-5033
Phone: 1-800-842-1508
TDD/TTY: 1-800-842-4524
E-mail: ctelderlyserv.dss@po.state.ct.us
Website: www.ctelderlyservices.state.ct.us

LTC Ombudsman
Address same as above.
Phone: 860-424-5200

Fax: 860-424-4966

Delaware
Delaware Health & Social Services
Div. of Services for Aging & Adults with Disabilities
1901 North Dupont Highway
Admin. Bldg., First Floor Annex
New Castle, DE 19720
Phone: 302-255-9390 or1-800-223-9074
Fax: 302-255-4445
Website: www.dsaapd.com

LTC Ombudsman
Address, phone, & fax same as above.
Website: www.dsaapd.com/ltcop.htm

District of Columbia
Office on Aging
Gov. of District of Columbia
One Judiciary Square
441 4th St., NW, Ste. 900 South
Washington, DC 20001
Phone: 202-724-5622
Fax: 202-724-4979
TDD/TYY: 202-724-8925
E-mail: dcoa@dc.gov
Website: www.dcoa.dc.gov/main.shtm

LTC Ombudsman
Legal Counsel for the Elderly
601 E St., N.W., A4-315
Washington, DC 20049
Phone: 202-434-2140
Fax: 202-434-6595

Florida
State of Florida, Dept of Elder Affairs
4040 Esplanade Way
Tallahassee, FL 32399-7000
Phone: 850-414-2000
Fax: 850-414-2004
E-mail: information@elderaffairs.org
Website:
elderaffairs.state.fl.us/doea/index.html

LTC Ombudsman
DOEA Ombudsman Program
Address same as above.
Phone: 888-831-0404
Fax: 850-414-2377
Website: www.myflorida.com/ombudsman

Georgia
Dept. of Human Resources
Div. of Aging Services
Two Peachtree St., NW, Ste. 9-385
Atlanta, GA 30303-3142
Phone: 404-657-5258
Fax: 404-657-5285
TTY: 404-657-1929
Website:
www2.state.ga.us/Departments/DHR/
aging.html

LTC Ombudsman
Office of the Georgia LTCO
Address same as above.
Phone: 888-454-5826
Fax: 404-463-8384
Website:
www2.state.ga.us/Departments/dhr/aging.html

Hawaii
Hawaii Dept. of Health
Executive Office on Aging
250 South Hotel St., Rm 406
Honolulu, HI 96813-2831
Phone: 808-586-0100
Fax: 808-586-0185
E-mail: eoa@health.state.hi.us
Website: www2.state.hi.us/eoa

LTC Ombudsman: Same as above.

Idaho
Idaho Commission on Aging
3380 American Terrace, Ste. 120
Boise, ID 83706
Mailing Address: PO Box 83720
Boise, ID 83720-0007
Phone: 208-334-3833
or toll-free: 877-471-2777
Fax: 208-334-3033

LTC Ombudsman
Address & phone same as above.
www.idahoaging.com/programs/ps_mbuds.
htm

Illinois Main Office
421 East Capitol Ave., Ste. 100
Springfield, IL 62701-1789
Phone: 217-785-3356
Fax: 217-785-4477

Illinois Chicago Office
State of Illinois Center, Ste. 10-350
100 West Randolph St.

Chicago, IL 60601
Phone: 312-814-2630
Fax: 312-814-2916
E-mail: ilsenior@aging.state.il.us

LTC Ombudsman
Address same as above.
Phone: 1-800-252-8966

Indiana
Indiana Family & Social Services Admin
Office of Communications
P. O. Box 7083
Indianapolis, IN 46207-7083
Phone: 1-800-986-3505

LTC Ombudsman: Same as above.

Iowa
Iowa Dept. of Elder Affairs
Clemens Bldg.
200 10th St., 3rd Floor
Des Moines, IA 50309-3609
Phone: 515-242-3333 or 800-532-3213
Fax: 515-242-3300
TTY: 515-242-3302

LTC Ombudsman: Same as above.

Kansas
Kansas Dept. on Aging
New England Bldg.
503 S. Kansas Ave.
Topeka, KS 66603-3404
Phone: 785-296-4986 or 1-800-432-3535
TTY: 785-291-3167
Fax: 785-296-0256
E-mail: wwwmail@aging.state.ks.us

LTC Ombudsman
900 SW Jackson St., Ste. 1041
Topeka, KS 66612
Phone: 785-296-3017
Fax: 785-296-3916
Website: http://da.state.ks.us/care

Kentucky
Office of Aging Services
275 East Main St.
Frankfort, KY 40601
Phone: 502-564-6930

LTC Ombudsman: Same as above.

Louisiana
Governor's Office of Elderly Affairs
412 N. 4th St., 3rd Floor
P.O. Box 80374
Baton Rouge, LA 70898-0374
Phone: 225-342-7100
Fax: 225-342-7133

LTC Ombudsman: Same as above.

Maine
Bureau of Elder & Adult Services
11 State House Station
442 Civic Center Drive
Augusta, Maine 04333
Phone: 207-287-9200
Fax: 207-287-9229
TTY: 207-287-9234 or 888-720-1925

LTC Ombudsman Program
1 Weston Court
P.O. Box 128
Augusta, ME 04332
Phone: 207-621-1079
Fax: 207-621-0509

Maryland
Maryland Dept. of Aging
301 West Preston St., Ste. 1007
Baltimore, MD 21201
Phone: 410-767-1100 or 1-800-243-3425
Fax: 410-333-7943

LTC Ombudsman: Same as above.

Massachusetts
Executive Office of Elder Affairs
The McCormack Bldg.
One Ashburton Place, 5th Floor
Boston, MA 02108-1518
Phone: 617-727-7750 or 1-800-243-4636
TTY: 1-800-872-0166

LTC Ombudsman
Address same as above.
Phone: 617-727-7750
Fax: 617-727-9368

Michigan
Michigan Office of Services to the Aging
P.O. Box 30676
Lansing, Michigan 48909-8176
Phone: 517-373-8230
Fax: 517-373-4092
TDD: 517-373-4096

LTC Ombudsman
State LTC Ombudsman
Elder Law of Michigan
221 N. Pine St.
Lansing, MI 48933
Phone: 517-485-9393 or 866-485-9393
Fax: 517-372-6401

Minnesota
Minnesota Board on Aging
444 Lafayette Road North
St. Paul, MN 55155-3843
Phone: 651-296-2770 or 1-800-882-6262
Fax: 651-297-7855
E-mail: mba@state.mn.us

LTC Ombudsman
Office of Ombudsman for Older
Minnesotans
121 East Seventh Place, Ste. 410
St. Paul, MN 55101
Phone: 1-800-657-3591
Fax: 651-297-5654

Mississippi
Div. of Aging & Adult Services
Mississippi Dept of Human Services
750 N. State St.
Jackson, Mississippi 39202
Phone: 601-359-4929 or 1-800-948-3090
Fax: 601-359-4970

LTC Ombudsman: Same as above.

Missouri
Missouri Dept. of Health & Senior Services
P.O. Box 570
Jefferson City, MO 65102
Phone: 573-751-6400
Fax: 573-751-6041

LTC Ombudsman
Missouri Div. on Aging
P.O. Box 1337
Jefferson City, MO 65102
Phone: 1-800-309-3282
Fax: 573-751-8687
Website:
www.dss.state.mo.us/da/ombud.htm

Montana
Senior & Long Term Care Div.
111 North Sanders, Rm. 210
Helena, MT 59604
Phone: 406-444-4077 or 1-800-551-3191
Fax: 406-444-7743

LTC Ombudsman: Same as above.

Nebraska
Div of Aging & Disability Services
State Unit on Aging
P. O. Box 95044
Lincoln NE 68509-5044
Phone: 402-471-4623 or 1-800-942-7830
Fax: 402-471-4619
Website: www.hhs.state.ne.us/ags/ltcombud.htm

LTC Ombudsman: Same as above.

Nevada
Div. for Aging Services
3100 West Sahara Ave., Ste. 103
Las Vegas, NV 89102
Phone: 702-486-3545
Fax: 702-486-3572
E-mail: dasvegas@aging.state.nv.us

LTC Ombudsman
445 Apple St., #104
Reno, NV 89502
Phone: 775-688-2964
Fax: 775-688-2969

New Hampshire
NH DHHS Div. of Elderly & Adult
Services
Long-Term Care Ombudsman
129 Pleasant St.
Concord, NH 03301-3857
Phone: 603-271-4680 or 1-800-351-1888
TDD: 1-800-735-2964
Fax: 603-271-4643

New Jersey
NJ Dept. of Community Affairs
101 South Broad St., PO Box 800
Trenton, NJ 08625-0800
Phone: 609-292-6420 or 1-877-222-3737
Fax: 609-984-6696
E-mail: DCA.feedback@dca.state.nj.us

LTC Ombudsman
Office of Ombudsman for Institutional
Elderly
P.O. Box 807
Trenton, NJ 08625-0807
Phone: 609-943-4026
Fax: 609-943-3479

New Mexico
New Mexico Aging & Long-Term Care
Dept.
228 E. Palace Ave.
Santa Fe, NM 87501
Phone: 505-827-7640 or1-800-432-2080

1410 San Pedro NE
Albuquerque, NM 87110
Phone: 505-255-0971 or 866-842-9230

2407 W. Picacho, Ste. B2
Las Cruces, NM 88005
Phone: 505-647-2023 or1-800-762-8690

LTC Ombudsman
New Mexico State Agency on Aging
228 East Palace Ave.
Santa Fe, NM 87501
Phone: 505-827-7663
Fax: 505-827-7649

New York
Albany County Dept for the Aging
112 State St., Rm. 710
Albany, NY 12207-2069
Phone: 518-447-7179
Fax: 518-447-7188

New York LTC Ombudsman
New York State Office for the Aging
2 Empire State Plaza, Agency Bldg. #2
Albany, NY 12223-0001
Phone: 518-474-7329
Fax: 518-474-7761

North Carolina
2101 Mail Service Center
Rm. 634
Raleigh, NC 27699-2101
Phone: 919-733-3983
Fax: 919-733-0443

LTC Ombudsman: Same as above.

North Dakota
Dept of Human Services
Aging Services Div.
600 S 2nd St, Ste. 1C
Bismarck, ND 58504-5729
Phone: 701-328-8910 or 1-800-451-8693
TDD 701-328-8968
Fax: 701-328-8989
E-mail: dhsaging@state.nd.us

LTC Ombudsman: Same as above.

Ohio
The Dept. of Aging
50 W. Broad St., 9th Fl.
Columbus, OH 43215-3363
Phone: 614-466-5500 or 614-644-7922
TTY: 614-466-6190
Fax: 614-644-5201

LTC Ombudsman: Same as above.

Oklahoma
Aging Services Div. OK Dept.
P.O. Box 25352
Oklahoma City, OK 73125
Phone: 405-521-2327
Fax: 405-521-2086

LTC Ombudsman
Aging Services Div. OK Dept
312 NE 28th St.
Oklahoma City, OK 73105
Phone: 405-521-6734 or 1-800-211-2116
Fax: 405-521-2086

Oregon
Oregon Dept of Human Services
Seniors & People with Disabilities
500 Summer St. NE E02
Salem, OR 97301-1073
Phone: 503-945-5811 or 1-800-282-8096

LTC Ombudsman
3855 Wolverine NE, Ste. 6
Salem, OR 97305-1251
Phone: 503-378-6533
Fax: 503-373-0852
Website: www.teleport.com/~ombud/

Pennsylvania
Dept. of Aging
555 Walnut St., 5th Floor
Harrisburg, PA 17101-1919
Office: 717-783-1550
Fax: 717-783-6842
E-mail: aging@state.pa.us

LTC Ombudsman
Address same as above.
Phone: 717-783-7247
Fax: 717-772-3382

Puerto Rico
Office on Aging
Governor's Office of Elderly Affairs
Commonwealth of Puerto Rico
Call Box 50063, Old San Juan Station

San Juan, PR 00902
Phone: 787-721-6121 or 809-721-5710
Fax: 787-721-2919

LTC Ombudsman
Address same as above.
Phone: 787-725-1515
Fax: 787-721-6510

Rhode Island
Dept. of Elderly Affairs
John O. Pastore Center
Benjamin Rush Bldg. #55
35 Howard Ave.
Cranston, RI 02920
Website: www.dea.state.ri.us/

LTC Ombudsman
Alliance for Better Long Term Care
422 Post Road, Ste. 204
Warwick, RI
Phone: 401-785-3340
Fax: 401-785-3391

South Carolina
Dept. of Health & Human Services
Office of Aging
P. O. Box 8206
Columbia, SC 29202-8206
Phone: 803-898-2500
E-mail info@dhhs.state.sc.us

LTC Ombudsman
Address same as above
Phone: 1-800-868-9095
Fax: 803-898-4513

South Dakota
Dept. of Social Services
Adult Services & Aging
700 Governors Drive
Pierre, SD 57501-2291
Phone: 605-773-3656 or 866-854-5465
Fax: 605-773-6834

LTC Ombudsman: Same as above.

Tennessee
Commission on Aging & Disability
500 Deaderick St., 9th Floor
Nashville, TN 37243-0860
Phone: 615-741-2056 or 866-836-6678
Text: 615-532-3893
Fax: 615-741-3309
E-mail: tnaging.tnaging@state.tn.us

LTC Ombudsman: Same as above.

Texas
Dept. on Aging
4900 N. Lamar Blvd, 4th Floor
P.O. Box 12786
Austin, TX 78711
Phone: 512-424-6840 or 1-800-252-2412
Fax: 512-424-6890
Website: www.tdoa.state.tx.us

LTC Ombudsman: Same as above.

Utah
Utah Div. of Aging & Adult Services
120 North 200 West, Rm. 401
Salt Lake City, Utah 84103
Phone: 801-538-3924
Fax: 801-538-4395

LTC Ombudsman: Same as above.

Vermont
Agency of Human Services
Dept. of Aging & Disabilities
103 South Main St.
Waterbury, VT 05671
Phone: 802-241-2400

LTC Ombudsman
Vermont Legal Aid, Inc.
264 N. Winooski
P.O. Box 1367
Burlington, VT 05402
Phone: 802-863-5620
Fax: 802-863-7152

Virginia
Dept. for the Aging
1600 Forest Ave., Ste. 102
Richmond, VA 23229
Phone: 804-662-9333
Voice/TTY: 1-800-552-3402)
Fax: 804-662-9354
E-mail: aging@vdh.state.va.us

LTC Ombudsman
Virginia Assn Area Agencies on Aging
530 East Main St., Ste. 428
Richmond, VA 23219
Phone: 804-644-2923
Fax: 804-644-5640
Website: www.vaaaa.org/longterm.html

Washington
Dept of Social & Health Services
Aging & Disability Services Admin
P.O. Box 45130
Olympia, WA 98504-5130
Phone: 1-800-737-0617 or1-800-422-3263
TTD: 1-800-737-7931
Website: www.aasa.dshs.wa.gov

LTC Ombudsman
South King County Multi-Service Center
1200 South 336th St.
P.O. Box 23699
Federal Way, WA 98093
Phone: 253-838-6810
Fax: 253-815-8173
Website: www.ltcop.org/index.htm

West Virginia
Bureau of Senior Services
1900 Kanawha Boulevard, East
Holly Grove, Bldg. #10
Charleston, WV 25305-0160
Phone: 304-558-3317
Fax: 304-558-0004

LTC Ombudsman: Same as above.

Wisconsin
PO Box 7851
Madison, WI 53707-7851
Phone: 608-266-0554

LTC Ombudsman
Wisconsin Board on Aging & Long Term
Care
214 North Hamilton St.
Madison, WI 53703
Phone: 1-800-815-0015
Fax: 608-261-6570

Wyoming
Aging Div.
6101 Yellowstone Rd., Rm. 259B
Cheyenne, WY 82002
Phone: 307-777-7986 or 1-800-442-2766

LTC Ombudsman
Wyoming Senior Citizens, Inc
756 Gilchrist, P.O. Box 94
Wheatland, WY 82201
Phone: 307-322-5553
Fax: 307-322-3283

Appendix 3—Online Resources for Older Adults in the U.S.

FirstGov for Seniors (administered by the Social Security Administration) is a portal website that contains extensive information on resources for seniors and dozens of links to relevant websites.
www.seniors.gov

National Aging Information Center
www.aoa.gov/NAIC/Notes/olderadults.html

Top Ten Senior Sites
www.top10links.com/Society/Seniors/Resources/Index.shtml

ConnectNew (Directory of locations for free access to internet)
www.connectnet.org/english

Resources for Developing User Friendly Sites for Older Adults

Older Adults and the World Wide Web: A Guide for Web Site Creators (Spry Foundation)
www.spry.org/WebGuide/WebGuideForm.htm

Creating Senior-Friendly Web Sites (Center for Medicare Education)
www.medicareed.org/pdfs/ibvln4.pdf

Making Your Web Site Senior Friendly (National Institute on Aging)
www.nlm.gov/pubs/checklist.pdf

Web Site Development for the Aging Network: Online Resources (U.S. Administration on Aging)
www.aoa.gov/webresources/default.htm

GeroTech
www.gerotech.com

The New Universal Service: NTIA's Guide for Users (National Telecommunications and Information Administration)
www.ntia.doc.gov/opadhome/uniserve/univweb.htm

Online Educational Programs for Seniors

Active Adult Training Program Directory
www.agelight.org/trainsites/trainingsites.htm

Senior Net's Educational Programs
www.seniornet.org/edu.shtml

Online Computers and Technology Resources for Seniors
AARP
www.aarp.org/comptech

Internet Sites for Older Adults

A2Z
www.seniorhospitality.com

AARP
www.aarp.org

Access America for Seniors
www.seniors.gov

Age of Reason
www.ageofreason.com

AgePage.Com
www.agepage.com

Ageless LifeStyle Magazine
www.agelesslifestyle.com

Double Nickels
www.doublenickels.com

Elderhostel
www.elderhostel.org

ElderNet
www.eldernet.com

Fifty Something.Net
www.50something.net

Fifty Plus Friends Club
www.50plusfriends.com

Friendly for Seniors
www.friendly4seniors.com

Generations Online
www.generationsonline.org

Our Senior Years
www.oursenioryears.com

Retire.net
www.retire.net

Retired.com
www.retired.com

Retirement Net
www.seniorsearch.net

(The) Seasoned Citizen
www.seasonedcitizen.com

Senior Circle
www.seniorcircle.com

Senior.Com
www.senior.com

(The) Senior Center
www.senior-center.com

Senior Citizens Gazette
www.senior-gazette.com

Senior Cyber Friends
www.seniorcyberfriends.com

Senior Focus Radio
www.seniorfocusradio.com

Senior Friendly
www.seniorfriendly.com

Senior Globe.com
www.seniorglobe.com

Senior Journal
www.seniorjournal.com

Senior Living
www.seniorliving.about.com

Senior Net
www.seniornet.org

Seniorresource.com
www.seniorresource.com

Senior Search Com
www.seniorssearch.com

Seniors on Line
www.seniors-on-line.com

Seniors-Site.Com
www.seniors-site.com

Seniors Surfers
www.seniorsurfers.org

Senior Surfers
www.seniorsurfers.com/index.html

Senior Women Web
www.seniorwomen.com

Third Age
www.thirdage.com

Yahoo Senior Guide
www.seniors.yahoo.com

Appendix 4—Elder Resource Organizations

AARP—American Association of Retired Persons, 1909 K Street N.W., Washington, D.C. 20049. 202-728-4200
> This nonprofit organization works to meet the needs of older people throughout the nation. They offer a wide range of publications and services for people over 55.

Caregiver Education and Support Project Extension Service, Oregon State University, Milam Hall 161, Corvallis, OR 97331. 503-737-3211
> This project has developed educational pamphlets for family caregivers, providing information in an easy-to-read fashion. Videos and other educational tools are also available for national distribution at cost.

Elder Care Locator, 1-800-677-1116
> This national toll-free number is designed to help identify community resources for seniors anywhere in the United States. The name, address, and zip code of the person needing assistance allows the Elder Care Locator to identify the nearest information and assistance sources in that person's community. Call between 9:00 a.m. and 8:00 p.m. Eastern Time.

Gray Panthers, 2025 Pennsylvania Ave., N.W., Ste 821, Washington, D.C. 20006. 202-466-3132
> This coalition of intergenerational activists works to promote the concerns of older people, often organizing around issues that cross age groups.

National Council of the Aging, 600 Maryland Ave., S.W., West Wing 100, Washington, D.C. 20004. 202-479-1200
> A private, nonprofit group serving as a central resource for information, technical assistance, training, planning, and consultation in gerontology.

National Council of Senior Citizens, 1331 F Street, N.W., Washington, D.C. 20004. 202-347-8800
> Composed of representatives of senior organizations throughout the nation, this group focuses on education and social action.

National Resource Center on Health Promotion and Aging, 601 E Street, N.W., Ste B5, Washington, D.C. 20049.

Publishes a bimonthly newsletter, "Perspectives in Health Promotion and Aging," containing updates on health issues of interest to caregivers.

Older Women's League, 730 11th Street, N.W., Ste 300, Washington, D.C. 20001. 202-783-6686

OWL's national membership is committed to helping meet the special needs of middle-aged older women, especially in areas such as Social Security, pension rights, health insurance, and caregiver support services.

Appendix 5—Sample Emergency Medical Form

The author wishes to thank Paul Grucza, CMCA, AMS, PCAM, of Consolidated Community Management, Inc., AAMC, in Tamarac, FL, for providing this sample form, which he has developed and used successfully with senior and other communities. Always have your association counsel review any form before using it for your community association.

Date _____

Contact Information

Name _____

Address _____

Other address(es) _____

Tel. #(s) _____

E-mail (if applicable) _____

Emergency contact(s) and relationship _____

Address(es) _____

Tel. #(s) _____

Medical Information

Age _____

Date of birth _____

Blood type _____

Primary care physician _____

Address _____

Tel. #(s) _____

Medical conditions that you think we should be aware of:

1. _____

2. _____

3. _____

Medications you are currently taking:

1. _____

2. _____

3. _____

Medical equipment you currently use:
1. _____
2. _____
3. _____

Other special instructions for our office:
Do you have an executed and valid durable power of attorney or a living will about which you'd like us to be aware?
❏ Yes
❏ No

If so, where can it be located in the event of an emergency?
_____
_____

Confidentiality
Please tell us who, if anyone, is entitled to access the information contained in this emergency medical information sheet. (The management of the association will not divulge this information to anyone other than your community manager, support staff, and emergency medical personnel, unless otherwise authorized by you.)
_____
_____

Please read the following, sign, and return to our office as soon as possible:
I/we residing at the address listed above do hereby authorize and approve management to release the above medical emergency information to those people indicated above. I/we also authorize and approve management to contact those individuals listed as "emergency contact(s)," above, should the need arise during my occupancy at this association.

I/we release management from any liability or responsibility with the dissemination of same information.
Signature & date _____
Signature & date _____
Witness _____

Please return this form to our offices with your next maintenance payment. Thank you.

About the Author

Ellen Hirsch de Haan, J.D.
Becker & Poliakoff, P.A.
2401 West Bay Drive, Ste 414
Largo, Florida 33770-1941
727-559-0588
edehaan@becker-poliakoff.com

Graduated from Boston University (B.A.), Ellen Hirsch de Haan received her Masters Degree in Education from the University of Massachusetts at Amherst; and completed her law studies at the University of Miami School of Law. She is a member of the Florida Bar, the American Bar Association, and the College of Community Association Lawyers.

Ms. de Haan is a well-known spokesperson for community associations having appeared locally on many television news broadcasts and talk shows and nationally on ABC World News Tonight, A Current Affair, Inside Report, and on QVC/Home Shopping Network. In addition, she was a speaker at the 1999 Communities of Tomorrow Summit, a national dialogue on excellence in community design, governance, and management held in Washington, D.C., and she was a featured speaker at the 5th Annual Condominium Conference of the Canadian Condominium Institute and Association of Condominium Managers of Ontario, in Toronto.

In addition to being a past co-editor of and current contributor to her firm's *Community Up-Date* newsletter, Ms. de Haan has published numerous articles in *Probate & Property*, the magazine of the Real Property, Probate and Trust Law Section of the American Bar Association, the *Journal of Community Association Law*, *Elder's Advisor*, and the *Journal of Elder Law and Post-Retirement Planning*. Ms. de Haan is also a contributing editor for CAI's *Common Ground*, to which she has contributed extensively for over a decade.

Ms. de Haan has authored two books: *Aging in Place: The Emergence of Naturally Occurring Retirement Communities*, in 1998; and *Self-Management: A Guide for the Small Community Association*, in 2001, published by Community Associations Institute.

Ms. de Haan has lectured extensively, not only throughout Florida, but also nationally at conferences, professional meetings, and colleges and universities, as well as the National Community Association Law Seminar, several chapters of the Florida Institute of Certified Public Accountants, and annually, for her firm's Community Associations Workshops.

Ms. de Haan develops and teaches certified continuing education courses for Florida community association managers, and is a member of the national CAI teaching faculty, as part of the Professional Management Designation Program. She has developed curriculum materials, and trained the faculty members under a CAI contract with the state of Florida, to provide educational programs for cooperatives and condominium association board members and owners.

Ms. de Haan has sat on many national and local boards including the national Community Associations Institute (CAI), of which she is past president, and CAI Broward County Chapter, and the CAI Suncoast Chapter. Ms. de Haan is a member of the Board of Advisors of the University of Miami School of Law Institute on Condominium and Cluster Developments and the Board of Advisors for the *Community Association Management Insider* published by Brownstone Publishers, Inc.

In addition to serving as an officer of many organizations, Ms. de Haan has served on numerous task forces and committees including the committees to revise and rewrite the state of Florida license examination for community association managers and the study guide for the examination; the state of Florida Escalator Safety Task Force; the American Bar Association Committee on Condominiums, Cooperatives and Associations, and the national CAI Public Policy Committee, Strategic Planning Committee, and Public Affairs Council.

Ms. de Haan's service to Community Associations Institute has earned her CAI's Outstanding Volunteer Service Award (1994 and 2003), Author of the Year Award (1997-1998), and the Distinguished Service Award (2002).

Case Study

How Del Mesa Carmel Is Meeting the Challenges of Its Aging Population

By Arthur W. Brown

D el Mesa Carmel is an active, self-managed, senior adult community in Carmel, California, comprising 289 clustered condominiums built between 1967-72. Located on the Monterey Peninsula on the coast 120 miles south of San Francisco, it's home to about 420 people who are 55 and older. Del Mesa Carmel offers natural beauty, cultural amenities, golf, tennis, excellent beaches, and a mild year-round climate. Residents are also attracted to Del Mesa for its beautiful clubhouse, indoor swimming pool, arts and crafts center, lawn bowling and putting greens, 340 wooded acres with walking trails, fitness center, and recreational, social, and cultural activities. Additionally, it's close to all the recreational facilities in the general area.

Del Mesa has never provided a medical program or facility; and, indeed, it attracts seniors who aren't quite ready for a medical facility. Residents must seek medical support from the community at large; however, the Monterey Peninsula has no HMO provider. Assisted living and nursing homes are limited, and home nurses and care providers are in demand. There are no continuous care facilities within 100 miles, but there are three life-care facilities (with long waiting lists), and one congregate living devel-

---

Editor's Note: The Del Mesa Carmel, Carmel, California, senior community developed a comprehensive program aimed at addressing aging in place issues. The program encompasses assessing its needs, developing in-house services and activities, organizing committees, implementing a vigorous communications program, and analyzing health care cost factors. Mr. Brown's documentation of the Del Mesa experience is extensive. This case study is an abridged version that will give the reader an understanding of how Del Mesa achieved success and an appreciation of the nature of the task facing every community association. The program works for Del Mesa, but may not be suitable for another community. Please consult with the association attorney for questions on liability, areas of expertise, and statutory and documentary issues, which may impact any programs within your community.

opment with limited medical capability. Furthermore it's unlikely that an assisted living facility will ever be built in the Del Mesa area.

In 1997, long-time Del Mesa residents and leaders began to notice changes. Their neighbors and friends were getting older. They began to see wheelchairs, walkers, and canes in the community. Conversations about health and the future became more common than talk about golf, tennis, movies, restaurants...even politics. People were asking, "What's long-term care insurance?" "Do you have it?" "How much does it cost?" "Are you moving to a life-care facility?"

As a result, the board of Del Mesa Carmel appointed an ad hoc Health Care Study Committee to assess the symptoms and determine if the association should take any action as a result of their findings.

Mission

The committee was made up of interested association members; members with expertise in finance, insurance, law, psychiatry, and health services. Together they defined the committee's mission and objectives as follows:

- Conduct a resident outreach effort to learn of resident's future medical care concerns, needs, and interests.

- Establish a Health Care Decision Guide that would offer residents a comprehensive road map to enhance their understanding of key health care alternatives and help them outline a rational action plan for achieving a more secure and comfortable health care future.

- Pursue and create, if possible, care-connected resources to assist residents on a voluntary basis with their hospitalization, follow-on convalescent or home care, and administrative needs.

Objectives

- Determine the purpose of Del Mesa, and what level of service residents expect. Was it a part-time get-away? Or an interim facility before moving to a nursing home? Had residents planned their futures? Did they need information or help to make plans?

- Protect the association from becoming closely involved in the personal lives of the residents, and be careful not to be responsible for their decisions. Provide information and referrals for assistance without making decisions for residents.

- Provide residents with information to evaluate alternatives and plan ahead; provide a list of resources about planning, medical assistance, administrative help, and custodial aid that would help them select satisfactory, cost-effective arrangements.

- Offer residents a health care strategy that provides access to quality in-home or institutional health care, and that offers various levels of services at competitive prices.

Concerns and Questions

Several questions and concerns about the task were raised:

- Will providing planning assistance and/or medical care:
  - encourage residents to reside longer in the community adding even more problems?
  - erode the community's image as a community for "active" seniors?
  - reduce the number of residents who were capable of or interested in serving on committees and the board of directors?
  - reduce the appeal of the community to younger homeowners?

- Is the effort to retain the community as an "active" community realistic in view of the increasing age of the adult population?

- Will the suggestions for the need for long-term-care insurance to cover in-home care cause more people to think of staying in the community longer than they plan on doing now?

- Will an aging and less active population be more conservative in the need to keep the facilities current and property values protected?

- Will a changing community demand more from the general manager and staff in knowledge and responsibilities if we expand into a more medically acute community?

- Will the association really be able to remain removed from any involvement in the medical care of the residents, i.e., can health care support for residents be achieved without association support?

- Are there care providers who can provide the kind of quality care required? Is it possible or appropriate for us to attempt to evaluate the quality of the programs of these providers (e.g., assisted living, nursing homes)?

Despite the significance of these questions, the committee decided to remove them from the table lest members be deterred and discouraged at the outset.

Resident Survey

In order to achieve the first objective, the committee designed and distributed a resident survey (see Case Study Appendix A) to which 49 percent of the residents responded. In addition, the committee conducted personal interviews with 30 percent of the survey respondents and conducted eight feedback sessions with small groups of residents.

Survey Results

- Most residents had moved into the community thinking it would be their last move.

- Nearly all residents loved and wanted to remain in the community as long as possible.

- The few who contemplated moving did so mostly due to health reasons.

- Of those who thought they'd leave, 50 percent were undecided about where they'd go, while nearly 30 percent would choose a life-care or continuous-care facility. Many were confused about the kinds of services each of these provided.

- The average age of residents had increased from 74 to 77 in three years and would conceivably continue to rise.

- Residents wanted the association's help in facilitating the guidance and coordination of their planning and emergency needs.

- Residents wanted to learn about and discuss with others their experiences with care providers, medical facilities, and medical services.

- Residents expected the community would provide a quality, safe, secure, and appropriate environment while they were in residency, and not after they were gone.

- Residents wanted a more active health and fitness program preferably on-site to help extend their life expectancy, only if this could be achieved at minimum cost.

- Most residents were not concerned about nor did they seem to comprehend the complexities related to the subject of mission or culture; however, they did not want the association to commit itself to any direct relationship with a care provider or to commit funds that might raise homeowner dues.

- Residents wanted the association to continue its study of health care issues.

After analyzing the survey responses and talking to most of the residents, it became obvious what lay ahead. The large majority wanted the association to become involved—they wanted guidance. Their health was becoming of more concern to them. And they were looking for answers they felt the association could help provide.

Dissent

A few residents expressed concern about any effort that might encourage residents to remain longer because it might result in an older population at Del Mesa. They felt this might slowly erode the community's original mission as an independent community for active seniors. A few wanted nothing to change, and they were concerned only about the present and their lifetime—not the future of the community.

Some residents questioned the advisability of having a health center on-site because it would clearly change the community's original mission. Nevertheless, the majority wanted a study that would look at all options for providing the community with an assisted facility either on or off-site—without committing the association to higher homeowner dues.

The Changing Face of the Community

As the committee studied the survey results, it saw very vividly the situation described in *Aging in Place*, written by Ellen Hirsch de Haan in 1998. Residents were healthier, more active, and independent; but, although they were living longer, they were experiencing a decline of physical ability and a gradual loss of strength, coordination, and mental acuity. This was affecting the quality of life, environment, and atmosphere of the community. The committee was convinced that the association simply had to become sensitive to the needs of its aging residents and ensure that its facilities, services, and programs were maintained and even altered to meet the health, safety, and security needs of all residents. In addition, residents needed guidance to their own future, and the committee felt this could be provided with little difficulty either directly or indirectly by the association.

The Committee's Formal Recommendations
Appoint a Standing Committee
The committee's first recommendation was to appoint a standing Life Care Awareness committee to initiate and maintain a sustained focus on health and life-care awareness among the residents of Del Mesa. The board accepted this recommendation and assigned the following duties to this new committee:

- Maintain a focus on the health and life care awareness and planning needs, interests, and concerns of the residents.

- Coordinate directly or support indirectly programs and activities that may serve the residents in matters related to their health and life care.

- Make residents aware of cost effective options and services that are available while they remain at Del Mesa.

- Monitor developments within the local area to help residents obtain the best health services available.

- Evaluate resident suggestions regarding health and life care matters and determine their merits.

- Work with staff and other committees to ensure that facilities and services meet the health, safety, and security needs of the residents.

Standing Committee Responsibilities
The standing committee members assumed responsibility—directly or indirectly—for various program areas.

- Work with the library association to establish and maintain a health and life awareness collection of reference books and periodicals.

- Develop a system for residents to exchange recommendations about care providers, health facilities, medical professionals, and other services.

- Create a list of professionals who will serve Del Mesa.

- Identify health and long-term planning topics suitable for seminars and lectures, and work with other committees to avoid overlap of subjects or speakers.

- Work with the Visiting Nurses Association or other comparable organizations to provide a nurses' clinic for an hour each weekday for blood pressure checks, other tests, personal counseling, etc.

- Maintain a close relationship with the three local care management organizations for the optimum benefit of the residents. Follow up with residents who are using the program to determine if additions to the program are needed.

- Coordinate volunteer rides for residents who require transportation for medical appointments.

- Conduct exercise and fitness programs, maintain the swimming pool, provide a meaningful fitness program for all interested residents, and make the most use of available facilities.

- Ensure that *A Guide to Your Personal Life Care Planning* is maintained, updated, and distributed to all residents.

- Keep residents up-to-date on all activities of the committee via the weekly calendar and the monthly newsletter.

- Monitor the medical community and help keep residents apprised of the most recent developments.

- Review Del Mesa's governing documents to determine if changes are needed.

- Conduct this effort without involving the association in any direct relationship with any agency or provider, and without leaving the association financially responsible for the medical expenses of any individual resident.

Develop a Life Care Planning Guide

The second recommendation was that the committee should compile available information and develop Del Mesa-specific information that would help residents with health and life-care planning. The resulting *Guide to Your Personal Life Care Planning* has been viewed by many as the principal product and most significant contribution of the committee. All residents receive a personal copy.

The *Guide* poses questions that help residents focus on financial planning issues; provides a directory of local resources; discusses insurance issues, including medical and long-term care, scope of coverage of Medicare, in-home care, Medigap coverage, Medicare coverage, care management, and emergency services; and provides a cost analysis and comparison of estimated costs for different types of care and facilities. (See Appendix B for an annotated list of these types of care facilities.)

For example, the *Guide's* section on financial planning encouraged residents to answer questions like:

- Will you have enough money to meet your future financial needs?

- Who will take care of your medical requirements?

- Where do you prefer to be in time of confinement and/or even up to and through your end of life?

To help answer these questions, the committee prepared a resident planning information form. (See Case Study Appendix C. Note that this is a planning tool and should not be confused with the Sample Emergency Medical Form shown in Appendix 4.)

Another example of the *Guide's* usefulness is its directory of local health care resources, which included a list of providers and costs for assisted living, health and medical care, in-home and off-site life-care and congregate living facilities, residential care homes, and skilled nursing facilities.

Other Committee Activities

In addition to developing the *Guide,* the committee was very active in numerous other areas.

For example, the committee writes a column for the community newsletter called "Life Care Awareness Update" that provides information on improving health, planning for the future, new developments in healthcare, medical programs, and obtaining various services at the lowest cost. Also, new programs and services developed by the committee are announced to all residents in a bulletin that becomes a part of the life care guide.

Major Accomplishments

- Obtained reduced prescription drug prices and free delivery to residents' homes—a service that was subsequently offered to other retirement communities in the area.

- Made arrangements for the on-site health clinic to provide additional services at no additional charge including basic first aid, blood sugar testing, coordination of referral and community services, home safety assessments, dressing changes, blood pressure checks, medication counseling, communication with personal physician, and Medicare clarification.

- Developed a directory of websites on subjects about various illnesses such as Alzheimer's Disease.

- Made arrangements for reduced member rates at a new full-service fitness center.

- Arranged for periodic counseling sessions for residents from Hi-Cap representatives on Medicare and insurance matters.

- Arranged for various alternative transportation resources to encompass the current Del Mesa van shuttle, obtained volunteer drivers for residents' medical appointments, reduced taxi rates for various destinations, and coordinated with the county transit system special fares for trips to shopping centers, hospitals, airports and the like.

Assessing Value

After three years of activity, the committee decided it needed to assess whether it was doing too much or too little. The committee believed it had fulfilled its original mission, but decided to conduct another survey to assess how effective it had been and to decide what to do next.

The survey was quite similar to the initial survey three years earlier. The only significant change was that 30 percent of the population had changed. The committee decided after factoring these statistics that it still had a valid base for reaching a meaningful conclusion.

Survey Responses

The responses confirmed what the committee had been doing was worthwhile.

- 97 percent of the respondents planned to remain at Del Mesa as long as they could.

- 81 percent of the respondents said they would leave because of failing health and the absence of a local health facility.

- 96 percent of respondents felt the committee had not been intruding into their personal lives.

- 92 percent of respondents reported the committee had actually helped them with their present and/or future health concerns and needs.

- 13 residents had purchased long-term care insurance and 19 had engaged a care manager because of the work of the committee.

- 50 percent of respondents credited the committee for getting them to exercise more.

- 84 percent of respondents supported the association's endorsement of an off-site assisted living facility (at no cost to Del Mesa).

Survey responses also allowed the committee to rank which of their activities had been most helpful to residents:

1. The life care guide
2. Newsletter updates
3. Education lectures
4. Resource directory
5. Resident exchange file
6. Health clinics
7. Fitness center upgrade
8. Volunteer rides
9. Prescription drug program
10. Exercise programs

The committee also reached a number of conclusions from its latest survey:

- The average age of the residents will continue to rise.

- Efforts to attract younger persons could and should be undertaken, but the association would have to take steps to offer them attractive amenities and lifestyles.

- The physical, emotional, and even financial status of the residents would continue to change; and, considering Fair Housing laws, the admissions criteria would become a critical matter.

- The number of invalid and in-home care residents would increase.

- The projected demographic shift is inevitable.

- The number of residents who would move into and remain in Del Mesa with the intention of having in-home care to the end of their lives would increase.

- The number of residents who would want continuously enhanced facilities would increase, and the number of resident wishing not to expend any association resources—regardless of the reason—would also increase.

- Property values would continue to be high.

- Older citizens would continue to be attracted to Del Mesa because of its location and appeal even though it does not offer medical assistance.

- The increasing complexity of issues and problems could eventually lead to the need for professional boards of directors.

- The association would benefit from having some sort of assisted living facility either on-site or nearby to accommodate the needs of the aging residents.

- The association should attempt to attract younger people by offering them fitness centers, computer rooms, cultural and social programs of interest to younger people.

- The association might eventually have to add staff to undertake tasks previously accomplished by volunteer committees.

- The association might eventually have to hire additional staff to assist the general manager in attending to the needs of an aging population.

New Projects

During the five years of the committee's existence, its importance has become obvious. Realizing this, the board gave its support for the committee to continue its on-going programs to increase the residents' awareness of available health-care options and services, pursue new services and programs that would be beneficial to residents in respect to their health-care needs, and recommend actions to the board that would help the association meet the aging in place challenges of the future. Thus, the committee proposed to undertake the following new projects:

- Arrange for a long-term care insurance "group" rate for residents.

- Encourage physicians to accept Medicare for Del Mesa residents.

- Negotiate reduced membership and playing fees for residents at local golf and tennis clubs.

- Investigate various technical applications such as knock-off phones, med-alert systems, automated call-in systems, and computer programs to serve residents' needs.

- Organize a volunteer friendship and support group that would help live-in residents.

- Provide support to developers who might consider building an assisted living facility nearby.

- Explore the possibility of arranging for a home-care organization to manage a network of Del Mesa homes whose residents require both care-providers and nurses.

- Develop a list of local merchants that would accept phone orders from and deliver groceries and meals to Del Mesa.

Obstacles to Implementation

Those committee members and community leaders who were associated with the program from its inception fully appreciate the obstacles and resistance they met. They included:

- Lack of understanding of what it meant to reside in an "independent living environment."

- Political issues and turf battles.

- Lack of long-range planning based on what the majority of residents expected.

- Resistance to change by long-term residents.

- Inability of residents and leaders to recognize the cultural changes.

- Inability of residents and leaders to take the cultural changes seriously.

- Inability of residents and leaders, who didn't plan to stay, to feel personally affected.

- Resistance from those who are interested only in what takes place during their lifetime, rather than what will benefit future residents.

Conclusion

It's one thing to understand what an aging population means to a community. But it's another matter to get residents—and even some community leaders—to respond.

Many changes implemented at Del Mesa have been made to create a safer and more secure environment and to update the governing documents to ensure their compliance with California and federal requirements. Fortunately, the association and its residents understand more clearly what challenges lie ahead for its aging population.

Its social, cultural, and recreational programs have all taken into consideration the aging profile of the residents. From a financial and organization posture the community is very nicely positioned for the future as far as can be envisioned. And new residents are being attracted to Del Mesa not only for its attractive setting, but also for its wonderful lifestyle.

Although Del Mesa is successfully adapting to its aging population, it should be remembered that a happy outcome can come only to those who, like Del Mesa, have planned ahead. The longer a community puts off planning, the fewer the available options and the greater their costs.

Case Study Appendix A—Resident Survey

Health Care Planning Study Resident Survey

As announced by the board of directors, the objective of the health care planning study is to:

- *Conduct a Residential Outreach Program to learn what future medical care concerns, needs, or interests residents may have.*

- *Establish a health care decision portfolio that will offer residents a comprehensive roadmap to enhance their understanding of the key alternatives and help them outline a rational action plan for achieving a more secure and comfortable health care future.*

- *Pursue and create, if possible, health care connection resources to assist residents on a voluntary basis with their hospitalization follow-on convalescent and/or home care, housekeeping, and administrative needs.*

The purpose of this survey is to fulfill the initial phase of the study. And, as a Del Mesan, your response is very important to our community. Only you can provide the committee with the information we need to define Del Mesa's overall wants, concerns, and interests.

We thank you for your assistance and time in responding to the following questions.

The Health Care Planning Committee

1. Number of people in your home?
   - ❏ One
   - ❏ Two

2. Number of years at Del Mesa? _____

3. Unless something unforeseen occurs, do you plan on remaining for some time at Del Mesa?
   - ❏ Yes
   - ❏ No

If you plan on moving, please indicate reason:
- ❏ Health
- ❏ Economic reasons
- ❏ To be closer to family
- ❏ Del Mesa is no longer meeting our needs
- ❏ Other: _____

4. Do you own another home that provides medical care assistance (e.g., Carmel Valley Manor)?
- ❏ Yes
- ❏ No
    If you do, please indicate the name: _____

5. Are you contemplating the purchase of such a facility in the near future?
- ❏ Yes
- ❏ No
    Please indicate where (optional) _____
    And when: _____
    Will you still retain your home at Del Mesa?
    - ❏ Yes
    - ❏ No

6. If you do feel you may leave Del Mesa for a facility that provides health care, please indicate what type of program interests you.
- ❏ Life care facility
- ❏ Rental with assisted care
- ❏ Nursing home
- ❏ Continuous care with equity
- ❏ Continuous care without equity
- ❏ Undecided

7. Do you plan on remaining at Del Mesa and having live-in home care as long as you can?
- ❏ Yes
- ❏ No

8. Do you have long-term care insurance?
- ❏ Yes
- ❏ No
    Please indicate what company you are with: _____

Are you interested in knowing more about this kind of insurance or need help in making a decision?

❑ Yes
❑ No

9. Do you have live-in care now?

❑ Yes
❑ No

Please indicate the following: _____

Number of hours per day: _____

Name of provider: _____

How long have you had this provider? _____ months

Please state services provided   Cost per hour/day

❑ Medical assistance   _____

❑ Administrative aid   _____

❑ Housekeeping   _____

❑ Other: _____   _____

Would you recommend this provider to others?

❑ Yes
❑ No

10. Do you have anyone handling your administrative needs (i.e., Medicare and health billing reconciliation, other bills)?

❑ Yes
❑ No

Approximate cost/month: _____

11. Do you have meals delivered to your home?

❑ Yes
❑ No

Please indicate by whom and when:

Indicate what days:

	Mon	Tue	Wed	Thu	Fri	Sat	Sun
Flying Owl	❑	❑	❑	❑	❑	❑	❑
Meals on Wheel	❑	❑	❑	❑	❑	❑	❑
Other	❑	❑	❑	❑	❑	❑	❑

Can the association do anything to help you in respect to this type of meal service? Please comment:

_____

_____

_____

12. Are you on any of the following?
Del Mesa morning check-in
❑ Yes
❑ No
Community Hospital Lifeline
❑ Yes
❑ No
If you are, are they satisfactory?
❑ Yes
❑ No
Please comment on your answer:

_____

_____

_____

13. Do you belong to an HMO?
❑ Yes
❑ No
If yes, please indicate the following:

Name

❑ Medical _____
❑ Dental _____
❑ Physicians Group _____
❑ Prescription Drugs _____
❑ Eye Care _____
❑ Other _____

14. Do you use a ride program?
❑ Yes
❑ No
If yes, please indicate which one(s)
❑ Rides of Monterey County
❑ Del Mesa Program
❑ Carmel Foundation
❑ Other: _____

15. Would you be interested in having the association develop a relationship with an assisted living and/or skilled nursing facility in the local area?
    ❑ Yes
    ❑ No
    ❑ Please comment to support your response:

    _____
    _____
    _____

16. Please indicate if you'd like to know more about any of the following:
    ❑ The difference between the various care facilities
      (e.g., continuous care vs. life care, or those in which you can
      acquire equity vs. rental only).
    ❑ Medicare coverage (especially the new revisions)
    ❑ Health insurance plans (i.e., for long-term care)
    ❑ Home equity loans
    ❑ The Eldercare Network
    ❑ Lifeline
    ❑ Adult day services
    ❑ Alliance on Aging programs
    ❑ Alzheimer's Association services
    ❑ Tele-Care program
    ❑ Care provider services for:
      ❑ Medical
      ❑ Housekeeping
      ❑ Administrative
    ❑ Other: _____

17. Would you be agreeable to discussing your own personal experiences and medical needs with a member of the committee to help provide us with specific insights?
    ❑ Yes
    ❑ No
    If yes, please provide your name and phone number in response to question #22.

18. How interested are you in having the association make an effort to help with your health care planning needs?
    ❑ Very interested
    ❑ Somewhat interested
    ❑ So-so

❏ Not too interested
❏ Very opposed to it

19. How optimistic are you that the association can help with your
    planning needs?
    ❏ Very optimistic
    ❏ Somewhat optimistic
    ❏ Not very optimistic
    ❏ Not optimistic at all

20. Do you have any concerns/problems about your own health care we
    have not covered in this survey that you would like to add?
    ❏ Yes
    ❏ No
    Please comment if you answered yes:

    _____
    _____
    _____

21. Additional comments and suggestions:

    _____
    _____
    _____
    _____
    _____

22. Name of residents (optional)
    Last: _____ First: _____
    Last: _____ First: _____
    House number:_____
    Phone: _____

*Thank you for your cooperation in completing the survey. We apologize for its length.
However, we simply believe the information we have asked for in the depth requested is needed
if we are to fulfill our task to the degree desired.*

Please return your completed response to the office no later than March 23rd.

The Healthcare Planning Committee

Case Study Appendix B—Types of Care Facilities

Assisted Living Facilities: Provide regular assistance with such daily tasks as eating, bathing, dressing, walking, and toilet functions.

Home Care Providers: Offer a wide variety of non-medical personal services (assisted living) to enable seniors to live comfortably in their homes as long as possible. Home care agencies are not licensed, but many employ state-certified nursing assistants or certified health aides. Medicare does not reimburse for home care. But most long-term care insurance policies do offer this option.

Hospice Care: Support for people with terminal illness. Medical care focuses on relieving pain, managing symptoms, and preserving the quality of life rather than prolonging life.

Home Health Care Providers: Provide medical services such as nursing, therapy, and nutritional advice. They are licensed by a State Department of Health and offer services in coordination with the patient's attending physician. Medicare will reimburse fees when the physician orders skilled nursing and when health care is provided by an agency certified by Medicare.

Skilled Nursing Facilities: This category includes convalescent hospitals and nursing homes. They provide licensed nursing and custodial care for patients convalescing from a serious illness or surgery. Many accept patients with mental impairments including Alzheimer's. Medicare usually covers funding for the initial 100 days. A few facilities provide hospice care.

Care/Case Management: Agencies that develop, plan, and implement a health care program that is directed to meet a person's short- and long-term health needs.

Congregate Living Facilities: Retirement apartments for rent where meals, housekeeping, laundry, and other amenities are available to ambulatory seniors. Residents enjoy an independent lifestyle without having to experience the pressures of home ownership. Residents generally pay monthly rental fees and a security deposit for accommodations and services. Some programs provide help with daily activities such as dressing and bathing from assisted living centers. For a fee, in addition to the monthly rate, residents may have an option for long-term care insurance for skilled off-site nursing care.

Continuing Care Communities: This type offers graduated levels of care: independent retirement living, assisted living, and skilled nursing care. Residents pay an entrance fee and varying monthly fees based on the level of care they need. The contract can cover one or more levels of care, either for the duration of a resident's life or for a term beyond one year, in exchange for an entry and monthly fee. In most cases, the entry fee is non-refundable, but some communities offer prorated plans, whereby residents or their heirs may receive a percentage of the entrance fee if they leave.

Continuing Care Communities With Equity: This type of facility allows residents to purchase homes with equity options and enjoy a health care program like a continuing care facility without equity. Some garner equity from the entry fee, and either give money back when a resident moves, or transfer money toward medical costs as needed. Health care services may be included in the monthly fee or may cost extra.

Life Care Communities: These facilities also provide independent living, assisted living, and skilled nursing care in one setting, but the entrance fee and monthly charges cover most types of care over a resident's lifetime. By law, life care communities must provide a full range of services, including access to nearby acute care and physicians and surgeons as well as skilled nursing.

Case Study Appendix C—Resident Planning Information Form

A planning profile for: _____

Notice

This Resident Planning Information Form is intended to contain information for the use of family and/or person responsible for handling the personal and medical matters of the resident as required.

This information should be regarded as confidential to any others than those given responsibility for assisting the resident in the time of need.

Name _____
             Last   *First*   *Middle*

Social Security Number _____

Address 1 _____
             Number   *Street*

_____
        City   *State*   *Zip*

Address 2 _____
             Number   *Street*

_____
        City   *State*   *Zip*

Telephone
1. _____ 2. _____

Drivers license _____ Birth date _____
Birthplace _____ Mother's maiden name _____

Marital status   Married _____ Single_____
Spouse/companion name _____

My children   Name   Address   Telephone

_____
_____
_____

Brothers/sisters

_____
_____
_____

Former occupation _____
Former employer _____
Employee Serial No. _____
Telephone   _____
Present employer if still working _____

My schools   Name   Address

_____
_____
_____

Organizations/Memberships   Name   Address/Contacts

_____
_____
_____

Religion _____ Church _____
Address _____ Telephone _____

Financial Information

A. Person responsible for handling my financial affairs should I
   become incapacitated.

_____
        Last   First   Middle

B. Documents executed to enable the above person to handle affairs:
   1. Type _____ Dated _____
   Location original _____ Location copy _____

2. Indicate any special provisions

_____

_____

_____

C. Bank(s)   *Name*   *Address*   *Account Numbers*

_____

_____

_____

Safe deposit no. _____ Key location _____

D. Insurance

Kind   *Policy Number*   *Company/Agent/Telephone*

Automobile   _____

Homeowners   _____

Disability   _____

Life   _____

Long-term care _____

Medical   _____

Other   _____

E. Investments (e.g., management firm, mutual funds, stocks and bonds, partnerships). Indicate kind, organization, advisor, and location of certificate(s).

_____

_____

_____

_____

_____

_____

F. Jewelry/other valuables and location

_____

_____

_____

G. Automobile(s) license numbers and location. Indicate where keys are located.

_____

_____

_____

H. Person who handles personal affairs/records

_____
Name   Address   Telephone

I. CPA

_____
Name   Address   Telephone

J. Location of tax returns (previous 5 years) _____

K. Attach statement of personal budget, including all income and expenses on a monthly basis.

Legal Matters

A. Attorney

_____
Name   Address   Telephone

B. Legal and estate planning documents/location
  1. Trust _____
  2. Will _____
  3. Durable power of attorney _____
  4. Uniform statutory form power of attorney _____
  5. Community property agreement _____
  6. Power of attorney for health care decisions _____
  7. Executor _____
        Name   Address   Telephone

C. Other important documents and location
  1. Birth certificate _____
  2. Employer insurance policies _____
  3. Automobile ownership certificates _____
  4. Marriage certificate _____
  5. Passport _____
  6. Credit cards   Name   Number   Location

_____

_____

_____

Pre-selected facilities (order of preference)

A. Hospital(s)

_____

_____

B. Skilled nursing facility

_____

_____

C. Residential care home

_____

_____

D. Home care agency

_____

_____

Funeral/Burial Request

A. Mortuary

_____

| Name | Address | Telephone |

B. Disposition _____ Internment _____
   Entombment _____ Cremation _____

C. Special instructions

_____

_____

_____

Advisors (other than attorney, CPA, executor):

                                   Name   Address   Telephone

A. Financial Advisor(s) _____

B. Stockbroker(s) _____

C. Insurance agent(s) _____

D. Physician(s) _____

E. Realtor _____

F. Clergy _____

G. Veterinarian _____

About CAI

America's leading advocate for responsible communities

Community Associations Institute (CAI) is the only national organization dedicated to fostering vibrant, responsive, competent community associations. Our mission is to assist community associations in promoting harmony, community, and responsible leadership. We believe that by giving board members, managers, and homeowners the knowledge to better run their associations, they can turn "owners" into "neighbors," increasing harmony, and leading to more prosperous, safer communities.

Putting the unity into community

CAI was founded in 1973 as a multi-disciplinary non-profit alliance serving all stakeholders in community associations. We provide education and resources to America's 231,000 residential condominium, cooperative, and homeowner associations, and to the professionals and suppliers who serve them.

CAI members include all types of association-governed communities, including condominium and homeowner associations, cooperatives, and planned communities of all sizes; individual homeowners; community managers and management firms; builders and developers; accountants, attorneys, lenders, insurance providers, reserve specialists, and other providers of professional services; public officials; and product and service suppliers—all working together to create more livable communities.

CAI has more than 16,000 members in 55 chapters throughout the United States and in several foreign countries, but our reach is much greater. Every homeowner in our member associations, and every employee in our member firms, enjoys many of the benefits of CAI membership as well.

The CAI Promise

In CAI, you'll find a friendly and accessible forum to develop relationships, increase your knowledge, and help shape the future of our communities. CAI offers a host of resources that will help you excel.

To find out more about CAI, visit www.caionline.org or call CAI Direct at 703-548-8600 (M–F, 9:00–5:30 ET).

About the Author

Kenneth Allan received his Ph.D. in sociology from the University of California, Riverside (1995), and is currently Associate Professor of Sociology at the University of North Carolina at Greensboro (UNCG). Before moving to UNCG, he directed the Teaching Assistant Development Program at the University of California, Riverside, and coedited *Training Teaching Assistants*, 2nd edition, published by the American Sociological Association. He has also published several works in the area of theory, including the 1998 monograph, *The Meaning of Culture*, and the more recent text, *Explorations in Classical Sociological Theory: Seeing the Social World*.

DATE DUE			

MAY -- 2018

LEGENDARY LANDFORMS
RIVERS

by Rebecca Pettiford

Ideas for Parents and Teachers

Pogo Books let children practice reading informational text while introducing them to nonfiction features such as headings, labels, sidebars, maps, and diagrams, as well as a table of contents, glossary, and index.

Carefully leveled text with a strong photo match offers early fluent readers the support they need to succeed.

Before Reading

- "Walk" through the book and point out the various nonfiction features. Ask the student what purpose each feature serves.

- Look at the glossary together. Read and discuss the words.

Read the Book

- Have the child read the book independently.

- Invite him or her to list questions that arise from reading.

After Reading

- Discuss the child's questions. Talk about how he or she might find answers to those questions.

- Prompt the child to think more. Ask: Have you ever been to a river? Where was it? What kinds of things did you see and do there?

Pogo Books are published by Jump!
5357 Penn Avenue South
Minneapolis, MN 55419
www.jumplibrary.com

Library of Congress Cataloging-in-Publication Data

Names: Pettiford, Rebecca, author.
Title: Rivers / by Rebecca Pettiford.
Description: Minneapolis, MN: Jump!, Inc., [2017]
Series: Legendary landforms | "Pogo Books are
published by Jump!" | Audience: Ages 7-10.
Identifiers: LCCN 2016051686 (print)
LCCN 2016051836 (ebook)
ISBN 9781620317099 (hard cover: alk. paper)
ISBN 9781620317417 (pbk.)
ISBN 9781624965869 (e-book)
Subjects: LCSH: Rivers–Juvenile literature.
Landforms–Juvenile literature.
Amazon River–Juvenile literature.
Classification: LCC TD392 .P48 2017 (print)
LCC TD392 (ebook) | DDC 551.48/3–dc23
LC record available at https://lccn.loc.gov/2016051686

Editor: Kirsten Chang
Book Designer: Leah Sanders
Photo Researcher: Leah Sanders

Photo Credits: lcrms/Shutterstock, cover; aphotostory/
Thinkstock, 1; RudyBalasko/Thinkstock, 3; Songquan
Deng/Shutterstock, 4; Max Topchii/Shutterstock, 5; Carl
Bruemmer/Getty, 6; karamysh/Shutterstock, 7; Vladimir
Melnikov/Shutterstock, 8-9; Steve_Bramall/Thinkstock,
10-11; Blake Kent/Getty, 12-13; Anton_Ivanov/
Shutterstock, 14-15; tbradford/iStock, 16; Erik Sampers/
Getty, 17; Florian Kopp/Alamy, 18-19; Kevin Schafer/
Minden Pictures, 20-21; VlLevi/Shutterstock, 23.

Printed in the United States of America at
Corporate Graphics in North Mankato, Minnesota.

TABLE OF CONTENTS

CHAPTER 1

FLOWING WATERS

Have you ever been to a river? Many of the world's largest cities are located close to one. These **landforms** give us fresh water to drink.

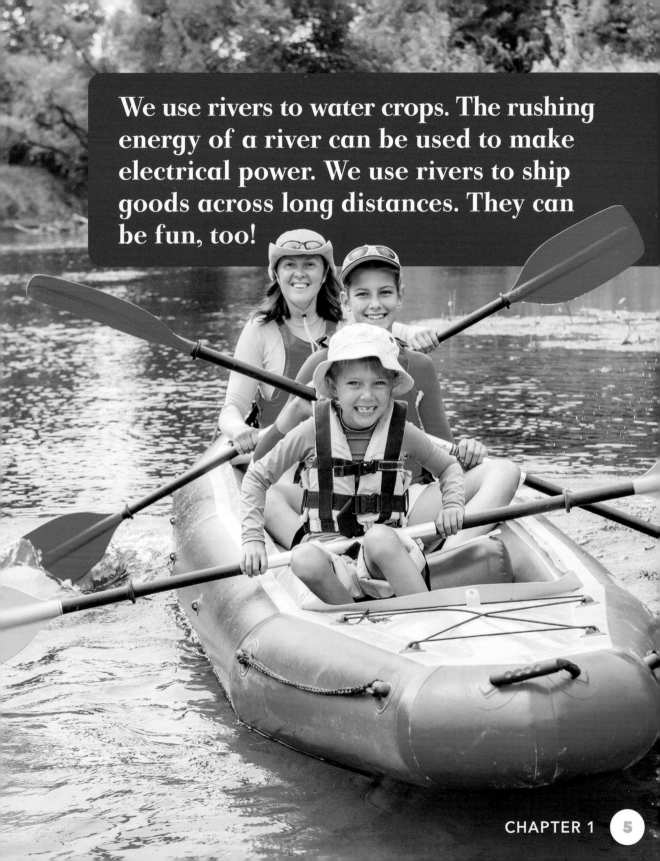

We use rivers to water crops. The rushing energy of a river can be used to make electrical power. We use rivers to ship goods across long distances. They can be fun, too!

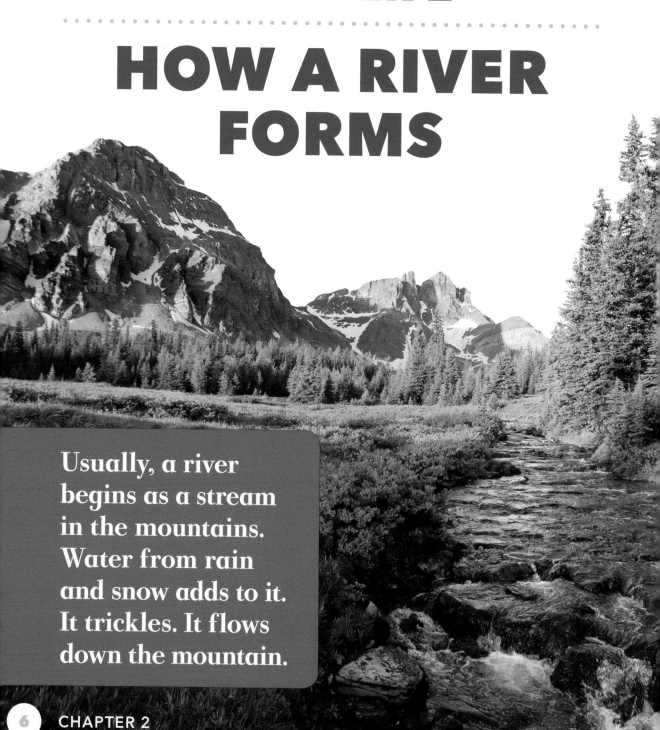

CHAPTER 2

HOW A RIVER FORMS

Usually, a river begins as a stream in the mountains. Water from rain and snow adds to it. It trickles. It flows down the mountain.

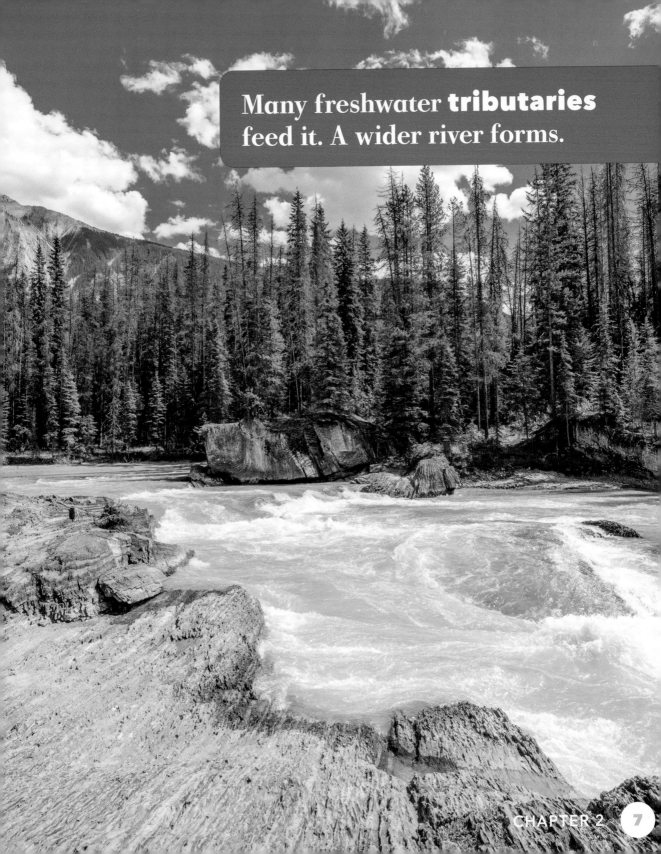

Many freshwater **tributaries** feed it. A wider river forms.

As a river flows, it carries **sediment**. It carries rocks and pebbles. The larger material is called the river's **load**. The river's load **erodes** the river channel. It makes it deeper. A river's channel is the path it takes across the land.

DID YOU KNOW?

The United States has more than 250,000 rivers. The longest is the Missouri River. The deepest is the Mississippi River.

riverbank

The land at the river's edge is called the **riverbank**. Flowing water erodes the riverbank. The river gets wider. Soil, rocks, and plant life also affect the river's shape.

DID YOU KNOW?

A river can be dangerous. When a river floods, it can harm crops and property. Powerful river rapids and currents can be deadly.

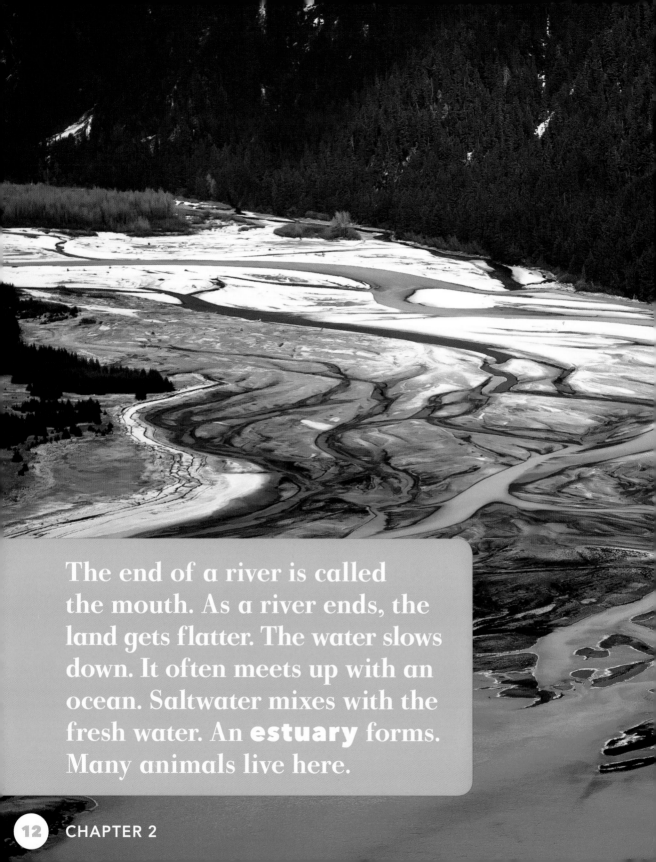

The end of a river is called the mouth. As a river ends, the land gets flatter. The water slows down. It often meets up with an ocean. Saltwater mixes with the fresh water. An **estuary** forms. Many animals live here.

What are the different parts of a river?

SOURCE

TRIBUTARY

CHANNEL

RIVERBANK

MOUTH

ESTUARY

Rivers shape the land through erosion. They cut out valleys and canyons. Millions of years ago, the Colorado River cut away layers of rock. In time, the Grand Canyon was formed.

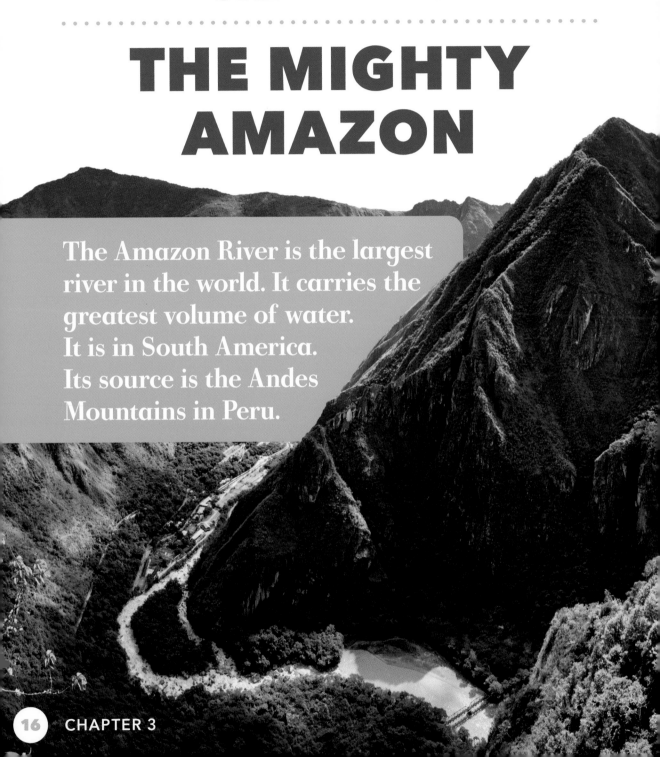

CHAPTER 3

THE MIGHTY AMAZON

The Amazon River is the largest river in the world. It carries the greatest volume of water. It is in South America. Its source is the Andes Mountains in Peru.

It flows through several countries. It is about 4,000 miles (6,400 kilometers) long. During heavy rains, the Amazon River is over 30 miles (50 km) across in places.

Why is the Amazon River so big?
It is located at the **equator**.
This warm area gets more than
33 feet (10 meters) of rain each
year. A lot of rain falls onto the
land around the river. This land
is called the Amazon basin.

The basin acts like a shallow dish.
Rain flows to the lowest part of the
dish. This is the Amazon River.

WHERE IS IT?

The Amazon River flows west to east through South America.

■ = Amazon River

river dolphin ·····▶

A river **cruise** is a fun way to explore this legendary landform. You can see all kinds of wildlife along the Amazon River!

DID YOU KNOW?

The Amazon River is home to electric fish, **manatees**, and river dolphins. Piranhas live here, too. These fish may eat small mammals!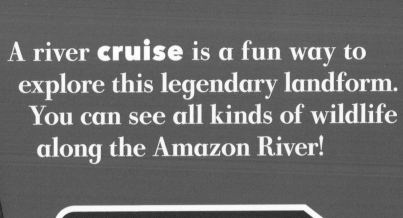

ACTIVITIES & TOOLS

RIVER LOAD ACTIVITY

A river can erode land and change its shape. But its power depends on the load it picks up and carries to sea. This activity will show you the power of a river's flow.

What You Need:

- a large glass bowl
- a wooden spoon
- 1 cup of coarse sand
- 3 cups of water

❶ **Place the sand in the bowl.**

❷ **Pour in the water.**

❸ **Stir quickly with the spoon. Do not touch the sand with the spoon.**

❹ **Notice that the moving water moves the sand around.**

❺ **Take out the spoon. Let the water rest.**

❻ **The larger bits of sand should sink first.**

❼ **As the water slows down, the smaller bits settle. Only moving water can carry away the sand.**

GLOSSARY

cruise: A trip on a boat or ship that is taken for fun.

equator: An imaginary line around the planet that divides it in half.

erodes: Destroys gradually.

estuary: An area where the river flows into the sea.

landforms: Natural features of Earth's surface.

load: Material, such as sediment and rocks, that is carried as a river flows.

manatees: Animals with flippers and a large, flat tail.

riverbank: Land at the edge of a river.

sediment: Material, such as stones and sand, that sinks to the bottom of a river.

tributaries: Smaller streams that feed into a larger river.

INDEX

TO LEARN MORE

Learning more is as easy as 1, 2, 3.

1) Go to www.factsurfer.com

2) Enter "legendaryrivers" into the search box.

3) Click the "Surf" button to see a list of websites.

With factsurfer, finding more information is just a click away.